OPUS DEI

Exploding a myth

by W.J. West

LITTLE HILLS PRESS

© W.J.West, 1987

Mount series is an imprint of
Little Hills Press Pty. Ltd.,
Regent House,
37-43 Alexander St.,
Crows Nest NSW 2065
Australia

Tavistock House,
34 Bromham Road,
Bedford. MK40 2QD
United Kingdom

Photographic credits:
W.J. West, A. Mullins, Information Office of the Prelature of Opus Dei,
Australia.

Cover design by Hand Graphics.

ISBN 0 949773 75 1

Reprinted 1988

Typeset by Midland Typesetters
Production by Vantage Graphics
Printed in Singapore

CONTENT

DEDICATION

to my parents.

1

ITALY
Opus Dei's secret

ROME, March, 1986. Few people in the eternal city during that month could have been unaware of the allegations. Newspapers around the country carried the story. Opus Dei stood accused of being a secret society. The organisations's 80,000 members were allegedly governed by secret statutes. Opus Dei was said to be the Catholic Church's version of the outlawed P2 Masonic Lodge. A coalition of anti-clerical elements in the Italian Parliament called for the Government to ban the organisation.

The incident began with allegations in the radical L'Espresso magazine. Several similar journals followed suit. It was clear to many observers that this trial by media amounted to little more than a campaign of slander. But the moves in Parliament which followed were more serious. They began with a series of questions about the nature of Opus Dei. The thrust of the claims was that Opus Dei had a hidden political agenda, that its "secret rules" required members to pledge obedience in all things and that members were required to keep their membership hidden.

The confrontation had been brewing for years. For some time a number of commentators had been employing the vocabulary of political intrigue and international espionage in articles about Opus Dei. But when you analysed the articles, when you removed the rhetoric, little remained beyond the assertion that Opus Dei was a secret society.

Throughout it all, Opus Dei insisted its members' political views were their own, that it was purely a spiritual organisation administering to peoples' spiritual needs. It had no political agenda. It did not even have any teachings of its own, but merely adhered to the teachings of the Roman Catholic Church. Some people accepted these explanations. Others refused to and promoted the idea that Opus Dei was politically motivated.

The sensational stories about Opus Dei began to appear soon after a young priest, Don Josemaría Escrivá, founded Opus Dei in Spain in 1928. One of the first allegations, made before a public inquiry, was that Opus Dei was the Jewish branch of Freemasonry. But the political image did not gain real currency until the late 1950s when members became ministers in the Spanish Government. In the 1960s the most prominent, often referred to as the "two Lopez", were Sr Gregorio Lopez Bravo and Sr Laureano Lopez Rodo. Both men held several Cabinet posts but made their biggest impact in the ministries of industry and planning. They were widely credited with engineering Spain's economic miracle, their work earning them the label "the technocrats". Another Opus Dei member in the Government, Sr Vicente Mortes, was a Falangist minister of housing.

All these men maintained that their political involvements had no connection with Opus Dei, that they acted independently and with complete freedom in their professional lives. Nevertheless the idea spread that Opus Dei was trying to take over the Government of Spain. The problem with the theory was that many members of Opus Dei opposed the Government. Some were jailed for political reasons. Others were expelled from Spain. An example was the publisher of the newspaper, Madrid, Sr Calvo Serer, whose newspaper was suspended for opposing the Government of which Sr Lopez Rodo and Sr Lopez Bravo were members. Sr Calvo Serer was exiled. However, all of this was less well known than the fact that three Opus Dei members were in the government. That fact alone stood out in the public consciousness.

The attack launched on Opus Dei in Rome in 1986 was different from previous ones. It was clear the matter was coming to a head. Prominent figures in public life were taking sides. Many well-known anti-Church elements, people who had only recently failed to have religious education removed from Italian schools, spoke against Opus Dei. One critic was Franco Bassanini, a former leader of a Catholic association who later joined the ranks of groups opposed to the Church. He also became a member of Parliament. Among those who came to the organisation's defence were the leader of the Christian Democrats, Flaminio Piccoli, and the Vice-President of the lower chamber of the Parliament, Guiseppe Azzaro. It was clear that the material already published had cast a shadow over Opus Dei's reputation and several parliamentarians urged the Government to act quickly to settle the matter.

As it turned out the Government decided to treat the claims seriously. The Minister of the Interior, a former lawyer and judge, Dr Oscar Luigi Scalfaro, announced that he would investigate and make a full report to the Parliament. The claims about Opus Dei were at last to be put to the test.

While awaiting the outcome I was to carry out some of my own investigations in Rome. . .

On the south-west side of Rome, a place where few tourists venture, a group of young boys emerged from a badly run-down apartment building and began to wander aimlessly along the pavement. One ran a lump of wood against a wall, then pounded it against some wooden panels overhead. Two more sat in a doorway, one crying, the other staring out at the littered street with its graffiti and yellowing political posters. Washing lines criss- crossed the apartment buildings. A home-made banner screamed: Risanamento immediato! Risanamento totale! (Renovate now! Renovate completely!).

This was Tiburtino. The poor came here from the south of Italy, from Sicily, Calabria, Abruzzo looking for a share of industrial wealth. Some found employment and improved their finances, but most found themselves living in soulless apartment buildings with little community life. The young children search out a vacant spot in a car park to kick a soccer ball. The older ones look for other ways to release their tensions—in one block there were three hypodermic syringes discarded on the footpath.

It is in this neighborhood that Opus Dei has established Centro ELIS. The soccer and basketball fields of the ELIS sports centre swarmed with youngsters. Alongside stood a youth hostel, a trade training school and a training centre for technical teachers from developing countries including Nigeria, Ethiopia and China. A women's centre, SAFI (Scuola Alberghiera Femminile Internazionale), operates a residence, a training centre for hotels, businesses and domestic work, a sports complex and a club for girls.

Tiburtino is a traditional communist stronghold. I asked one of the founders of the ELIS centre, Dr Bruno Picker, if Opus Dei had ever been accused of playing politics at ELIS. "When we started all the people around were waiting for us to make political propaganda," Dr Picker said. "But Opus Dei doesn't do this. It just gives Christian formation and after that everyone is free. After two or three elections passed and people saw we did not do anything they began to accept that we really did not have political goals. Many of the communists in this area, which is about 50 per cent communist, appreciated what we were doing. They saw that ELIS took a professional approach and that we did not make politics. Some communists now send their children here. One man, an old builder who was one of Italy's first communists, approached us. He said he was interested in helping but first he wanted to look closely at our day-to-day activities and to go over our books. ELIS had not been completed, it was still growing and after he had looked into all aspects of it he told us he wanted to finish his life helping us finish ELIS. He gave us a great deal of money and insisted that he not receive any recognition for it."

Dr Picker spoke of Monsignor Escrivá's interest in the ELIS project. The founder of Opus Dei, he said, saw one of its functions as spreading the social doctrine of the church on questions like co-operation in industry, ownership of private property and the family. But Monsignor Escrivá had stressed that it was important to make it clear the people at ELIS were against no-one: "that we are not anti-communist, but are for the people, that we should not be throwing stones at others, but elevating them."

The reputation of the ELIS complex has grown steadily since it opened in 1964. It is now such that the project receives financial support from the local government, even when it is led by communists.

On January 15, 1984, during a visit to ELIS, which had by then seen 18,000 youths take part in its programmes, Pope John Paul II commented: "This centre is a clear witness of the Church's interest in the working classes." He quoted Pope Paul VI's words at the centre's inauguration: "This is a work of the Gospel, it is not a mere hotel, a mere workshop or a mere school, it is not just any athletic field: it is a centre where friendship, trust, happiness, create an atmosphere; where life has its dignity, its meaning, its hope; it is the Christian life which is here affirmed and lived out. . ." It was on this same pastoral visit that John Paul II exhorted the members of Opus Dei to "become Opus Dei more and more", adding: "and may you carry out Opus Dei in all directions of the human world and the world of created things."

It was Saturday and in a central square children of all ages were playing, watched by mothers who sat talking on nearby steps. Many parents had come to watch their children play sport. Mr and Mrs Marchetti had a 10-year-old son, Maximilian, who had been coming to ELIS Sports Centre for a year. His parents said ELIS taught him manners and moral principles. "Every month the children are asked to concentrate on a new aim, like generosity or sportsmanship," Mr Marchetti said. "In a poor neighborhood like this nobody teaches the children these things." 'Our son has a tutor he can talk to about his problems," Mrs Marchetti added. "He has found out that other children have the same problems. They try to solve them together. He seems more mature since coming here and I notice he tries to help the other children." Mr Nicola had a 15-year-old son who played basketball. "When my son came here he always wanted to be the best, to always win. But he has learnt this is not the way to be," he said.

Another father said: "They teach the children how to get along with others, how to be friends, and that they must be active in everything, not just sport." One couple said their son had learnt to organise his time, to give time to study as well as soccer. Mrs Chiappini, a widow with three sons said her boys had learnt to think of the future. "Centro ELIS has helped them understand that it is very hard to get a good job in Italy and that they have to work hard," she said. "My eldest is now studying to be a mechanic at ELIS. I don't know what he would be doing otherwise." One mother spoke of two new programs ELIS was preparing to help young people cope with unemployment and to fight the spread of drug abuse in the area.

One of the basketball coaches at ELIS is Roberto Castellano. Roberto had been a captain of the Banco di Roma team which took out the Italian championships and, according to a sporting magazine, was one of Europe's most popular basketball players. Not long before we spoke he had declined an offer to further his basketball career by joining another team outside Rome. He said no because he wanted to continue teaching basketball to schoolboys in ELIS. This decision seemed to many of his countrymen extraordinary. One journalist asked if perhaps he had some psychological problem.

"Sport is important for the young," Roberto reflected. "First, to learn the spirit of sport, that there is something more important than winning—things like generosity and honesty and the rest. If a boy can live these in sport then probably he can live them in life. "When I was 19 I came to know of Monsignor Escrivá's teachings and I loved the spirit of Opus Dei, the spirit of work and apostolate. Opus Dei is new and to explain to those not practising their faith can be difficult. My friends only understand material things. So first of all I explain Opus Dei with my life and then I try to help the other person to find the way of Jesus Christ. Opus Dei is one of the ways in the Church. There are many but this is one—sanctification of work. Many of my friends work only for money. But I tell them it is important that they find Jesus in their life. Many think that Jesus is only inside the church, that he has no place outside it. I try to explain to them that they cannot live without God, that the reason for everything we do, for our whole life, is God."

It was Easter in Rome. Pilgrims were arriving from all over the world. Among them were thousands of students who had come to take part in the annual international university congress called UNIV. While UNIV is not an Opus Dei activity, many of those involved are Opus Dei members. The conference was organised by the Institute for University Co-operation (ICU), a group which works with the European Community and international organisations to train professionals all over the world, particularly from developing countries. The conference attracted 5000 students from 40 countries. During a wide-ranging speech to participants John Paul II spoke warmly of Opus Dei and its founder. The week-long gathering which followed was a mixture of formal conference sessions at the Conference Hall of Rome's Central

National Library and excursions around the historic sights of the city.

During a bus trip around Rome one Opus Dei member, Fr Michael Barrett, a straight-talking young American priest from the Bronx, spoke about his own involvement in Opus Dei. What did he think of the claims about Opus Dei and secrecy? "I think its a lot of nonsense frankly because it is very easy to find out whatever you want about Opus Dei," he said. "I don't think there is any friend of mine or even an acquaintance who did not know even before I became a priest that I was in Opus Dei or at least that I was trying to be a good Catholic in an environment in which not everybody was. When I was working in Wall Street secretaries, fellow workers, bosses, would all know that Barrett was a guy who tried to live his faith. Then the vast majority discover Opus Dei because it comes out in conversation."

Did priests ever speak to people about politics? "If anything I try to avoid speaking about politics. And it is frankly sometimes difficult. You're used to expressing your personal opinion because having been a layman for so many years you are politically involved and aware and on top of things. I can sense it very well that keeping out of political discussions entirely you will be more useful to people who need priestly guidance. People are looking for a priest to answer questions of their conscience that are really important things, things that they don't want just anyone to respond to. So if you talk about politics and have a political stand then you lose a lot of your effectiveness and so it is something that has always been insisted on about priests in Opus Dei that they not have anything to do with politics. A priest is perhaps somewhat of an expert in theology but not in politics. And yet if he does talk about politics some people will think he is an expert. So therefore he has got to take pains not to ever abuse the power that he has in his state by speaking about politics."

What approach would a priest of Opus Dei take when giving spiritual advice to someone whose profession was in politics—a member of a government for instance? "It would be spiritual advice which would have to do with his relationship with Our Lord. It would be spiritual advice having to do with the principles of morality as the Church teaches them. The rest is up to him in terms of applying the advice to his interior life, to try to get closer to Our Lord, to the sacraments, through prayer, through spiritual reading, spiritual classes and so on. As far as the moral principles go, it is up to his conscience to decide whether he wants to follow a certain path. Most politics is opinionable in any case. Whether the person is on one side of the fence or the other he is not doing anything that has to do with morality. It is outside of morality. Matters can be handled in more than one way. Maybe there are three or four. When it does touch on matters of morality the priest can explain what the principles of the Church are, what the Church has taught on certain things having to do with social doctrine. A priest of Opus Dei is not going to tell what political proposal best fits with some moral principle because a priest of Opus Dei would not know. He is not a politician."

How had Fr Barrett met up with Opus Dei? "It was through one of my friends who was a member. We used to do lots of things together, go to dances, double date and things like that and sometimes over a beer we would talk about the things that were important to us. He told me about what he did as a member of Opus Dei and bit by bit I began to do prayer, spiritual reading, go to Mass more than just on Sundays. I went along to a center of Opus Dei and I liked what I saw as friendly, cheerful people who were serious about work and study and particularly about their faith. There is a period where you begin to have interior life. There was a friend who suggested maybe I should be a member of Opus Dei like he was. It didn't seem out of the question for me from the point of view of my interests and what I was going to do with my life. I was studying at Columbia at that time. I had just moved into pre-medical. Before that I was majoring in science. The whole idea of sanctity in the middle of the world really turned me on. I thought it was fantastic.

"So Opus Dei was fantastic, the thought of becoming a doctor or whatever you wanted to become and that at the same time you could be striving to be a saint and helping others to become saints. In February 1972, I joined Opus Dei. "After I graduated from Columbia I took a job with the Gulf Oil Corporation in New York. I moved into an apartment with three others—a priest and two lay men— and we began a small center. Besides trying to help my friends and colleagues at work to live their faith better, in this small apartment we gave spiritual formation to men of all ages.

"My professional work was selling petrochemicals and what I learnt from Opus Dei helped me see the spiritual significance of what was a fairly worldly job. A lot of time was spent entertaining clients, which is why I moved on after a while. I mean two years of that was fun; it paid well, a nice expense account and all that, but you get a little bit tired of it.

"I was always fascinated by Wall St, though I knew very

little about it. The best way to learn was to find a job, so that is what I did. I got a position with the stock brokers, Merrill Lynch. I'd say the main thing in all of that was trying to see that there was a supernatural reason to the way I was doing things even though it was very ordinary and very worldly, and sometimes trying to help fellow workers get on track with their faith. I remember we had an office of four men. One was the manager and there were three of us salesmen. We were fairly close friends. We did a lot of work together, travelled at times together. I would have hours to talk to these guys. You passed evenings together when you were out of town. One was married with a family, a Catholic. He had a lot of questions and was maybe confused with the way things were done. Not sure himself about what it was all about, but trying very hard to be a good Catholic. We became very close friends. We talked a lot about what the faith was and with this guy I just tried to help him live his faith a little better.

"The other fellow was single and not a practicing Catholic. He had fallen away. We became good friends and I tried to help him to think about getting back to the Church. It was something he always wanted to do but some people just need help sometimes to do it."

"Then there were the clients. We would talk about things sometimes over lunch after we finished talking about business. We talked about sport, politics, religion—it always comes up. They would always be impressed to find that there was this possibility of trying to live your faith doing whatever you normally do. I suppose it was what you would call a spontaneous kind of apostolate, nothing very organised and most of these guys would think about going back to the sacrament of confession or about meeting a priest who would tell them how they could live their faith and answer some of their problems and questions.''

What about the claim some people had made that this sort of approach was ''instrumentalising'' friendship (that is using friendship merely as a means of getting others involved in Opus Dei)? ''Well everybody has his own way of being, but personally I have always had a lot of friends and some very good friends. Some guys I would consider so close they are like brothers and we continue to be friends even though the years have come and gone by and we are separated by distance. We would talk for hours about what we wanted to do with our lives and our dreams and our goals . . . and pushing each other along, saying: 'You can do it, I'm sure you will,' and that sort of thing. So fine, when I joined Opus Dei I continued the same pattern of making new friendships which developed through professional work and common interests and talking about things. I would talk about my things and one of my things is that I have put a lot of my life into Opus Dei and so to say I'm not going to talk about it would be ridiculous. It would be like someone else not talking for instance about some fabulous girl that they're dating.''

''So a friend might ask: 'How come you're not going to get married?' or: 'How come you spend so much time working with programmes for kids or organising things?' And when you explain what moves you to spend your time like this they are honestly happy you have this vocation, just like I'd be happy for them if they find a really good wife or they get the job they have been after or whatever.''

At this point the bus we were travelling in arrived at Villa Tevere where the central offices of Opus Dei are to be found.

OPUS DEI

Located at 75 Viale Bruno Buozzi, Rome, the villa is the official residence of the elected Prelate of Opus Dei, presently Monsignor Alvaro del Portillo. It is also the site of the church of the prelature of Opus Dei, Our Lady of Peace, where beneath a simple dark green marble stone with gold lettering which says simply El Padre, Monsignor Escrivá is buried. Visitors from all over the world file through, past dozens of fresh red roses, kneeling to kiss the marble and make their petitions. They are mothers, fathers, grandparents, single people and children, people of all social classes and all walks of life. The crypt of Our Lady of Peace has become a place of pilgrimage not only for members of Opus Dei, but for many others with a devotion to Monsignor Escrivá.

The founder of Opus Dei once outlined in a newspaper interview his attitude to the claims that Opus Dei was seeking political influence. "Opus Dei's influence in civil society is not of a temporal nature (social, political or economic); though it is reflected in the ethical aspects of human activities," he said. "Like the influence of the Church itself, the soul of the world, it belongs to a different and higher order and is expressed precisely by the word 'sanctification'. This leads us to the subject of the members of Opus Dei whom you call influential. In an association whose aim is political, those members will be influential who occupy positions in parliament or in government, in the council of ministers, in the cabinet. In a cultural association, the influential members will be philosophers of renown, or authors of national reputation, etc. But if, as in the case with Opus Dei, the aim is the sanctification of ordinary work, be it manual or intellectual, it is obvious that all members have to be considered influential because all of them work, and in Opus Dei the general duty to work carries with it special

20

disciplinary and ascetical significance. All of them endeavour to do their work, whatever it may be, in a holy, Christian manner, with a desire for perfection. For me, therefore, the witness which a son of mine who is a miner gives among his companions is as influential, as important and necessary, as that of a vice-chancellor of a university among the other members of the academic body.''

When the time came for me to leave Rome the Italian Government had not yet completed its inquiries into whether Opus Dei was a secret society. The task was to take more than six months. On November 25, 1986, the day after the minister presented his findings, the newspaper La Stampa summed up the result with the headlines: Opus Dei Is Not Secret, and: Duty Of Obedience Refers Exclusively to Spiritual Matters. Similar stories appeared in Il Tempo and La Republica. The article in La Republica quoted the minister as saying Opus Dei was not a secret association, neither as a matter of law nor as a matter of fact. He said that while no organisation was required to publish the names of members, the names of Opus Dei's directors had been published, as had the addresses of its centers and their activities. Members did not seek to hide their membership, he said. In fact they were forbidden to do so under the organisation's statutes. These statutes, which the minister quoted in detail, were what critics had claimed to be Opus Dei's secret rules. Before the secrecy claims arose the statutes, like those of other bodies in the Church, had not been published. However, to demonstrate that there was nothing to hide, the Prelate of Opus Dei approached the Vatican to have the statutes made public. The Vatican agreed and copies were made available. None of the critics took up the offer to examine them.

On the question of whether Opus Dei was seeking political power the Minister of the Interior found members had the same freedom as other Catholics in their personal affairs. To illustrate the point he read from article 88, paragraph 3 of Opus Dei's statutes which says the prelature does not make its own the professional, social, political, economic activities of any of the faithful and that "the authorities of the prelature must refrain totally from giving even advice in these matters." That these facts represented an accurate picture of how Opus Dei operated in practise was guaranteed by the Holy See, which stressed the fact that Opus Dei was now part of the constitutional structure of the Church.

The arguments the minister put before the parliament to support his finding that Opus Dei was not a secret society were lengthy and detailed. Anti-Catholic elements in the parliament offered nothing to contradict the facts. Did this mean Opus Dei would no longer be considered a secret soicety? At the time of writing the answer to this question is at least doubtful. For instance, in Australia the events which led to the Italian Government's investigation were reported at length. As far as I have been able to establish, the results of the Government's investigations were not reported at all.

Why should the secret-society image of Opus Dei be so resilient? As already mentioned, the publicity given to Opus Dei members in the Spanish Government in the 1960s has reinforced the idea that Opus Dei is political. This belief has been fueled by a more general suspicion that Catholics associate outside a church for mainly worldly reasons. After all there appear to be plenty of precedents. Catholic Action groups have been set up in the past to consider how Catholic teachings apply to concrete political situations. Some Catholics, particularly earlier this century in France and Italy, formed associations to defend themselves from anti-clerical groups or parties and set up "Catholic" unions, banks and credit unions. Is it not conceivable, the sceptics reason, that all this activity has simply gone underground and is being carried out by Opus Dei? Besides, if Catholics want spiritual help why go beyond their local parish? Thus when Opus Dei says its aims are purely religious, that members have complete freedom in other areas on their lives, the assertion has tended to fall on deaf ears. One thing alone is taken as given: Opus Dei is politically motivated.

For someone who believes this is true, it would seem legitimate to ask: "What then is Opus Dei up to?" After all you never see politicians declaring their Opus Dei credentials. You do not see Opus Dei contingents at public meetings. Nobody ever spells out the Opus Dei platform on any issue. It seems there can be only one conclusion, a fact set in stone for all time: Opus Dei is a secret society. In addition to those who really believe Opus Dei is political and a secret society the influence of those who oppose the Catholic Church on principle should not be overlooked. This group—anarchists, anti-clericals and so on—must necessarily feel threatened by any Catholic organisation with a large number of members in the professions, the media and business. Whether they believe their own propaganda or not, it is clearly in their interests to keep the scandal brewing, to sow suspicion and doubt about Opus Dei amongst Catholics and non-Catholics alike.

At this point the reader may be wondering what this writer's relationship is to Opus Dei. The answer is that at the time I began my research into Opus Dei I was considering becoming a member and was taking the first steps in that direction. As much as anyone I had a reason for wanting to know the truth about Opus Dei. I decided to travel around the world to interview members and look at the work they were doing. At the time of writing I have made a short-term commitment to Opus Dei.

In what follows I have not tried to water down the idealism of its members: the constant talk of seeking after virtue and the struggle to serve God and their fellow man. I have tried to give an accurate account of what I heard and saw.

Italy was the second stop on my journey, a journey which began when I flew out of the Australian summer in late February 1986 into a cold winter's day in Tokyo . . .

2

JAPAN
Spirit of discovery

THOUGH spring was near winter snow was still falling in Tokyo. The bullet train to Osaka was full of businessmen. There was little talk and no laughter. The passengers, even the girls who pushed trolleys of refreshments through the carriages, had a disciplined, military air. Why come to the land of the Samurai, of Buddha and Shinto in search of something Catholic? It was the idea that in order to really appreciate something it is important to try to see it as though for the first time. In Japan, most Opus Dei members were converts; they were not only seeing Opus Dei for the first time, but Christianity as well. So this was the attraction of Japan: finding out what people seeing Christianity for the first time were seeing.

OPUS DEI

At Osaka station there was a bar with multi-coloured plastic replicas of meals in the window. It seemed an unusual way to advertise food, but at least it overcame the language barrier. An unshaven cook was preparing meals behind the counter. He looked an unhappy man. Lines of care had formed on his face. His dark eyes told you he dreaded his job. A piece of meat fell from his wok and landed on the stove in front of him. He glanced over his shoulder for customers, reached out and tossed the morsel back in.

I considered how one would go about explaining Opus Dei to this man? The basic idea is summed up in a prayer for the beatification of the founder, Monsignor Josemaría Escrivá: "Opus Dei, a way of sanctification in daily work and in the fulfilment of the ordinary duties of a Christian'; in other words, a way to grow closer to God by doing everything, including your professional work, as well as possible. As Monsignor Escrivá explained it: "the miracle of turning the prose of each day into heroic verse by the love which you put into your ordinary work."

Outside the bar people were shopping. According to Monsignor Escrivá, even apparently mundane tasks like shopping could be turned into a form of Christian contemplation; God was everywhere and willing to reveal something through the smallest experiences.

In the early 1930s, when the founder of Opus Dei began to preach this idea that ordinary people could be contemplatives and seek spiritual perfection, not despite their daily work, but through it, the idea seemed radical to many people. The young priest was even branded by some of his contemporaries in Spain as a heretic. This happened even though there were many biblical texts which supported the claims he made. Theologians as far back as St Augustine had referred to it. But nobody, not even the monks for whom work was important, had built a spirituality around the work ordinary people do, and many found the idea hard to accept.

In Japan too, you would expect the idea would be novel. In the East they have always believed that if you want to seek spiritual perfection you go off to a monastery, or at least live apart from ordinary workers. The idea that someone with a family and a mortgage could pursue the same goal as a monk would be likely to appear every bit as unusual to a Japanese as it would to an Englishman.

Nevertheless the founder of Opus Dei, insisted on this point: "Contemplation," he said, "is not something for a privileged few. Some people with only elementary knowledge of religion think that contemplatives spend the whole day in ecstasy. But this shows great naivety. The monks in their monasteries are busy all day with a thousand tasks. They do the cleaning of the house and devote themselves to tasks by which they earn their livelihood. Religious, both men and women, leading contemplative lives, frequently write me, with great expectancy and with affection for (Opus Dei), saying that they pray a lot for us. They understand what many people do not, namely, our secular way of life as contemplatives in the middle of the world."

From Osaka I took another train to Ashiya to visit the Seido Language Institute. A four-storey building houses the institute. Its huge red sign is today one of the most visible landmarks in the mainly residential city. Seido began in the late 1950s when two priests, Father Ray Madurga and Father Fernando Acaso, and a handful of lay members of Opus Dei came to Japan. They came with no money, spoke little

Japanese and were unfamiliar with the culture. Founding a language school was a bold step. In all 15,000 students, young and old, of all religions and none at all, have now passed through and the language books published by Seido's printing section compete successfully in Japan with Oxford and Cambridge university presses.

A regular visitor at Seido was Yokoe Tomonori, a lawyer and former rugby footballer. Yokoe called in once or twice a week for lessons in the Catholic faith or for meditations given by one of the Opus Dei priests. He spoke of the spiritual journey which led him to become a Christian. "We Japanese have a word, Bushido, the code of the Samurai," he explained. "It stresses patience, willpower and endurance for the sake of becoming strong. I knew of these ideas, but struggling to be patient so I could be manly was not enough. When I learned you could offer this struggle to God, to sanctify yourself, it changed everything. I think this was what attracted me to Opus Dei: I learnt to find a meaning in the small details of my life. It was the idea that work had a special meaning, a value before God."

This idea of looking for God in the small things of life has a long history in the Church. It was something the medievals understood well—something reflected in the great cathedrals of Europe and the minutely detailed manuscripts of the middle ages. It is the romance of excellence, the idea that a divine spark can be found in the smallest details of life. And one of the most exciting aspects is that it can be a source of spiritual inspiration to everyone whether they are a biochemist or a bricklayer.

Another visitor at Seido was Kazuhico Eguchi, a middle-aged businessman who came into touch with Opus Dei while at school, but later lost contact. After starting a family, he decided to seek out the people he had met at Seido again. "I remembered their smiling faces . . . it is hard to say . . . I thought they had backbone," he said. "There was much in their eyes. More than the deep thoughts, what attracted me was the impression when I saw these people that inside there was something peaceful."

Like most Japanese, Kazuhico had always worked hard, but there had been no special purpose in it. "Number one was to get plenty of money and a high position in my company," he said, "but I could not get peace in my heart. After reading the writings of Monsignor Escrivá I found there were many other things in life. I learnt to love everyday life. Monsignor Escrivá said in this routine life it is very important to remember heaven is the final destination. I used to be very busy, too busy to worry about other people such as my family. But Opus Dei taught me that when you have order in your life and a purpose, time multiplies. Now I find I have time for my family and for other people as well."

Kazuhico's comment about time multiplying was something I had heard many others comment on. They said they seemed to get more done and their everyday tasks no longer seemed a burden. In doing even the smallest things as well as possible, in seeking after excellence, they had found themselves surprised by an unfamiliar joy.

Another visitor to Seido, Kiyoyuki Fuwa, had converted to Christianity after meeting up with Opus Dei. Like Yokoe he saw himself as a contemplative: a contemplative, he explained, with a wife and children to support. A sales manager when we met, Kiyoyuki came across Opus Dei in 1968. Earlier, as a law student at Kyoto University he had become involved with a radical movement and took to the streets with left-wing students in the "revolution" of 1968.

Later, at Seido he met another former student from his university, a member of Opus Dei named Koichi Yamamoto.

"Koichi spoke of God," Fuwa said. "I was an anarchist. My father was a Buddhist. I loved Koichi, but I had no thoughts of God."

Japanese culture and education, as Fuwa pointed out, does not involve an all-powerful God who created all things. While it is true that in Shinto there are many gods, there is not one who began everything and this, above all, made it difficult for Fuwa to appreciate what moved his friend Koichi. Still, he listened to what Koichi had to say and things happened to him which made him think more about God. Fuwa could not say what exactly inspired his conversion to Christianity, but his friendship with Koichi, who has since died, obviously had an effect. You could see it when his friend's name passed his lips.

Of Opus Dei Fuwa had this to say: "One reason for joining was this idea of work as a way of sanctifying myself. I had always hated my work and it made me very tired. But because of this new idea I tried to do my work well and then it became pleasant. I wasn't tired anymore. It went smoothly."

Fuwa added he had also learned to control his temper. "This is something I have to be careful about. When I feel angry I have to shut my mouth. I read about that in a book by Monsignor Escrivá, The Way; to have more patience and wait until the proper moment." He paused and then added with a grin: "Sometimes I have to shut my mouth for two or three days."

That the people at Seido were so candid about their lives was surprising. The Japanese have a reputation for being slow to express their feelings, especially to foreigners—part of what has come to be known as the "we Japanese" mentality. In fact it is said they have three hearts: one for friends, one for close relatives and the third, they say, the Japanese themselves don't even know.

Statistics show few Japanese actively practice any religion. Less than 1 per cent are Christian, partly the legacy of the period when Western influence was locked out of Japan. Eiko Iseki, a young woman who helped run an Opus Dei centre in Ashiya and who met Opus Dei while studying in London said before she went to England she could not believe anyone believed in God. "I always liked the idea of Jesus Christ, but I did not believe in God," she said. "When I went to the Opus Dei Centre I saw it was natural and I was impressed by the whole thing. The British are not so friendly, but at Dawliffe Hall everyone was very cheerful, very kind. That impression never died. They were always like that and I decided it was because of faith in God and this idea of offering everything you do to God.

"You see, we Japanese tend to be materialistic. We are successful, but it does not satisfy us. We work so much, but we don't know how to be happy. My mother, a Buddhist though she does not practice any religion, told me when I decided to become a Christian: 'We Japanese are very different from other people.' But that is not true. We are the same people and we need the same things. A lot of young people in Japan are looking for a standard to live by, which is not the product of other human beings. If you take time to talk to them and explain Christianity they respond. Many of my friends come to the centre here and have learned about looking for God in everything you do. Some are now faithful of the prelature."

OPUS DEI

Before my stay at Seido came to an end one of the teachers showed me around the institute. It was full of students of all ages. When Seido started there were only 16 of them squatting on tatami mats in a rented house. Over the years their numbers had grown to 1400. Attached to the institute is a residential wing, home to a small group of Opus Dei members, mostly numeraries and priests. Apart from the Japanese residents, there were several Brazilians, an American, a German, and two Spaniards. Some were teachers, others administrators, and some worked outside the language centre.

The residents lived a regular routine. They rose about 6.30, spent half an hour at prayer in the centre's chapel before hearing Mass. Some worked at the language school, others out in the community. At night the main spiritual activities were a further half hour of prayer and 15 minutes of spiritual reading. The residents lived much as any lay person with a job and a family would. They played sport, went out to dinner and on outings and so on.

From Ashiya I flew to Nagasaki, the cradle of Christianity in Japan on the southern island of Kyushu where the 26 martyrs died and where Christians survived more than two centuries of isolation and persecution. Just outside the city, between St Mary's Hill and the Hill of the Cross, looking down on the Valley of the Three Rivers, is the Seido school. Housed in neat, red, flat-roofed buildings at the end of a steep road that winds its way up from a deep valley, Seido is on a site which was previously unrelieved hillside. The "mountain" literally had to be moved to create enough ground to build the first buildings. Those who founded the school in 1976 had few resources and its success was a small miracle.

Only one third of the students at the school are Catholic. Though it began as a co-educational venture, it later separated into boys' and girls' sections. The schools seek to promote equality on all levels; hot meals are served in the canteen so the poorer children eat as well as their friends; uniforms are worn for the same reason. Fees are tailored to ability to pay and no-one is turned away for financial reasons.

Many of those who run Seido, but not all, are members of Opus Dei. One member, Saiki Tetsuya, worked with an interior decorating firm before he took a job managing the office of the boys' school. Leaving his company was a big step; for the Japanese the company is something which demands great loyalty. It was also unusual because members of Opus Dei normally remain in the same jobs they were in before becoming members. But Saiki said he was inspired by the ideas behind the Seido school and wanted to play an active role. Saiki took me home to meet his family his wife and their three young children and while we drank green tea, squatting at a low table, he explained how he had discovered Christianity through the writings of Monsignor Escrivá.

"Christianity was a new world for me," he said. "I thought Monsignor Escrivá's preaching was beautiful because I didn't change my life, but I was changed inside. Sometimes I think I was like St Paul after he met Jesus on the road to Damascus. My whole outlook on life changed."

At the time he met Opus Dei, Saiki was an administrator and he found the job difficult. "But I was helped by what I was taught by Opus Dei about offering your work to God, about looking for God in the small details, in doing things well and keeping order in your life. This spirit that I learnt was not just a matter of doing your physical work as well as possible, it also affected the way you treated fellow workers. I learnt in Opus Dei that you should have consideration and love for other people. Our Japanese companies can be very cold. The head of the section and the employees don't want to know each other more deeply. But I learned it was important to know more about the others as a friend.

During our conversation Saiki said he felt many Japanese placed material prosperity above everything else. This meant they often neglected having children. The subject of the family had been on my mind since my first night in Japan. The potential problems for families struck me forcefully at Tokyo station. It was about 9 o'clock and hordes of office workers, row after row of grey-coated men, swarmed into bars and restaurants to dine with their colleagues, before hurrying home to sleep. They were there again in the early hours, now headed in the opposite direction to their offices. Given that Japanese businessmen spend much of their time on weekends with business contacts, playing golf or at company functions, it was hard to see how they found time for their children. One young man in Ashiya confided to me sadly that he had never really known his father; when he grew up his father seemed like a stranger. This experience is not uncommon in Japan. For instance a government survey in 1987 showed only 40 per cent of Japanese children like their father. Twenty-eight per cent said their father's never took them for a walk or played games with them. On average fathers spent only 36 minutes a day with their children.

Today the family is under attack in many ways, but long before these threats arose, the founder of Opus Dei

34

recognised the importance of ordinary family life partly due to his own ability for seeing the greatness in the ordinary things of life, seeing them as though for the first time. He recognised in marriage and raising a family something of the deepest significance for the spiritual life of lay people. He stressed marriage was a "divine path", a vocation in the same way as the priesthood or the life of a religious was a vocation. The people at Seido were not merely interested in bringing lives into the world. They underlined the importance of each member of a family taking their role in the family seriously. As Monsignor Escrivá put it, the secret of good family life is "in everyday things, not in daydreams".

"It lies in finding the hidden joy of coming home in the evening," he said, "in affectionate relations with children; in everyday work in which the whole family cooperates; in good humour in the face of difficulties that should be met with a sporting spirit; in making the best use of all the advances that civilisation offers to help us bring up children, to make the house pleasant and life more simple."

"I constantly tell those who have been called by God to form a home to love one another always, to love each other with the love of their youth. Anyone who thinks that love ends when the worries and difficulties that life brings with it begin, has a poor idea of marriage, which is a sacrament and an ideal and a vocation. It is precisely then that love grows strong. Torrents of worries and difficulties are incapable of drowning true love because people who sacrifice themselves generously together are brought closer by their sacrifice. As Scripture says, a host of difficulties, physical and moral, cannot extinguish love."

Many people in Japan spoke of the sacrifices they had made for their families, things like buying a house near their offices to cut travelling time and finding extra time for the family on weekends.

Members of Opus Dei in Nagasaki said they believed spreading the joy of family life was one of the most important things they were trying to do. The principal of the Seido girls school, Miss Nakajima Kazuko, told of a woman who came to her one day with a new-born baby in her arms and said: "This is Seido's baby. Before I sent my other children to Seido I had decided not to have any more. But afterwards I realised what a beautiful thing it is to have children, and how happy they make you. And so I think of this one as Seido's baby."

Fukahori Eiji is a teacher at Seido, a jazz pianist and a member of Opus Dei. He took me to his home, a small timber cottage near a narrow canal where we spoke at length about Opus Dei and the effect it had had on his family. Fukahori spoke of the change in his attitude to having children: "I used to see them as a burden," he said, "but now I see them as a blessing from God. I don't worry either about whether we will be able to get by because I know since God has given me seven children it is impossible He will let me down."

Mrs Fukahori said her attitude had changed "180 degrees". Previously she had felt unhappy with her lot in life. "I didn't like being a housewife," she said. "My ideal was not life in the home. I thought it was a waste, mainly, I think, because this is what so many people told me. But in Opus Dei I learned that raising children and being at home was the most beautiful thing of all. Coming to realise that changed my whole outlook. I began to enjoy what I do as a wife and mother very much, particularly because I learnt to consciously offer it to God. That is not to say there are only joys in raising children. There are also disappointments. And this is where Opus Dei is a tremendous help. It gives me spiritual direction and I can open up. This is something I can find nowhere else."

Before I left the Fukahori household I was shown something written by Fukahori's 13-year-old son, Yoshihiki, a student at Seido. It was something he had composed for a public speaking contest.

"Today, I would like to talk about grandmothers and grandfathers," young Fukahori began. "Grandmas and grandpas, are you there? I am sure you are! You always watch us, your grandsons and grandaughters: our sleeping and waking, our meaningless talking and laughing, our growing up to be free and responsible men. In all these, there is joy in your heart. There is comfort. In the family we are 11: my father and mother, six brothers and sisters, my grandma and my grandpa. My father works all day and my mother usually stays at home. Four of us go to school every day. Grandma and grandpa work part of the day. We are just like any other family except perhaps for being a big family and also maybe for the presence of grandma and grandpa. They are really a big help to the family.

"On coming home, for instance, the first thing grandpa does is take a look at the baby and be with her for a while. He always sings the same song to her called Kita Kuni no Haru. The baby hears and hears it again and now she sings it together with grandpa. We hear the same song over and over again and now we sing it too. Everybody sings Kita Kuni no Haru in the family.

"My grandpa also has a small garden where he cultivates fruits and vegetables. He is very generous to the neighbors around and sometimes gives them part of the harvest. It's not seldom to hear our neighbors say thank you to him. At home, we share together the fruit he has gathered at the end of the day. As for my grandmother, she comes home tired. In spite of all that she helps my mother do the house chores without a word of complaint.

"On seeing them offer their lives in the small, 'unseen' sacrifice of each day, I'm filled with admiration and respect. Their example, more than their words is a constant encouragement. So here is to you grandmothers and grandfathers, a tribute of honour for all your silent sacrifice, for all the hardships you bore for our own good and well being. Thank you very much. I assure you, your effort will not go to waste."

It was a simple little story but it reflected something essential of the spirit of Opus Dei. Young Fukahori had captured something central to that spirit: the importance of ordinary working life and of struggling day after day to create a good environment for the family. Of course concern for the family is not peculiar to Opus Dei, or even to Christians. But Opus Dei does emphasise family life as a means to spiritual growth. It reminds lay people that it is not only by meditation in a quiet retreat that a person may go to God but also in a noisy living room surrounded by screaming children. In this sense, as in many others, Opus Dei is at its heart a celebration of the common person.

Towards the end of my stay with the Japanese, some words Saint Francis Xavier had written when he came to Japan in 1549, came to mind: "The people whom we have met so far are the best who have as yet been discovered . . . they are a people of very good manners, good in general, and not malicious; they are men of honour to a marvel and prize honour above all else in the world."

Given all this virtue, what could Christianity offer the Japanese? Many converts spoke of the things they most appreciated about their new-found faith and what it could offer the Japanese people. One man said he believed the Japanese were in many ways already Christian at heart and they thought they did not need Christianity; after all, many Christians seemed to lack the virtues they had. But he pointed out what the Japanese lacked was an awareness of centring their actions on God. Even if they had some understanding of God, for them God was not, as in the Christian sense, loving and loveable. Such concepts were difficult for the Japanese to understand. "They can understand that God is powerful," the man said, "but not that God is love and that you can go to him through the love you put into everything you do. This is something Opus Dei has helped me understand and it is something the Japanese need to be made aware of."

One woman mentioned the ability to cope with suffering. In eastern religions the search for a spiritual peace or quietude is absolute. Witness the many images of Buddha in repose, or meditating in peaceful solitude. Against this background human suffering is a real obstacle. The woman who spoke to me recalled the experience of her father who had died three years before. He had been a good man, a practising Buddhist with high moral principles. In many respects he did not feel the need for Christianity. But then he contracted cancer and suffered great pain. He kept asking over and over again why he had to suffer so much. He believed he had tried to be a good man and could not understand why he should have such pain. "It is the same for all of us," his daughter told me. "We all suffer in some way and we need an explanation of it. I don't think we can get that outside Christianity.

Whatever their special interests, the people I spoke to agreed with Mitsui Takeshi, an electrical engineer with Mitsubishi in Tokyo. He said the most important thing Opus Dei had to offer the Japanese was an understanding of contemplation in everyday life. "Generally we lay people cannot find the ideal way to Christianity," Mitsui said. "I think the concept of contemplation is difficult for the ordinary person, but it is necessary. First it is important to have order in your life, to plan to use the time well and secondly to have the spirit of contemplation during ordinary work and family life. Contemplation is intimacy with God, a conversation between God and me. It is something which is difficult, but attractive. Without it daily life becomes hard. But with it there is a constant sweetness, even when things are not going well."

So for the Japanese, discovering Christianity through Opus Dei meant discovering, along with everything else, the supernatural value of ordinary life. The essential thing was the commitment to being a contemplative in the middle of the world. This above all was what Monsignor Escrivá sought to do in founding Opus Dei: to open, not the only way, but one way for ordinary people to become contemplatives through their ordinary working lives.

The reaction of some people when told that they should offer their work to God seems to be: "Yes. What else?" But Monsignor Escrivá was continually telling such people: "Hold on, this is something important, something you should spend your whole life investigating and growing to appreciate more. For the ordinary person, work and all that goes with it is an essential part of the spiritual life.''

This conviction about ordinary work was shared by members of Opus Dei I met in countries around the world. In each one Opus Dei inspired something different. But it was always the same spirit, a spirit hard to express adequately in concepts or ideas. It was best illustrated by peoples' lives. Perhaps the best illustration of the spirit of Opus Dei is the life of the founder.

3

THE FOUNDER

JOSEMARÍA Escrivá de Balaguer was born at Barbastro, the main town of the Somontano region of northern Spain, on January 9, 1902. He was the second of the six children of Don Jose Escrivá y Corzan, a partner in a retail business, and his wife, Maria de los Dolores. The Escrivás are said to have been gentle and patient with their children, teaching by example and showing them how to live a Christian optimism in the face of adversity. Partly through the collapse of his father's business and the relative poverty which followed, Josemaría developed a strong character. As a youth, he is described as full of good humour, a good student and though devout, without any desire to become a priest.

Josemaría did, however, believe God wanted something from him. He said he had experiences, "intimations of love", which gradually opened his mind to what lay ahead. It was not until 1918 that he decided to enter the priesthood in order, as he said, to make himself available for whatever God wanted. At the same time he sensed what was being asked of him had to do with the life of ordinary lay people, rather than that of religious. He therefore took a civil law degree at the University of Saragossa at the same time as he studied for the priesthood. Later he would work as lecturer of philosophy and professional ethics at Madrid's School of Journalism and lecturer of Roman law in Saragossa and Madrid.

After being ordained in 1925, Don Josemaría passed short periods in country parishes and at Saragossa before moving to Madrid. While teaching Roman law and Canon law at Madrid's Cicuendez Academy, he gave much of his time to Madrid's poorest suburbs, Vallecas and Tetuan, visiting the sick in their homes and in hospitals. During these visits he asked those he was helping to pray for the task he believed God was preparing him to carry out. As he said later: "The human strength of (Opus Dei) has been the sick people in the hospitals of Madrid: the most forsaken ones; those who lived in their houses having lost the last vestige of human hope; the most ignorant in the remotest corners of the city."

It was on October 2, 1928, that the young priest finally knew what was expected of him. He said that during a retreat in a house for the Vincentians in Garcia de Paredes St, Madrid, he "saw" Opus Dei. The reality, now spread around the world, became clear in his mind.

He said later he did not like the idea of being the founder of anything. But he nevertheless set about, with a spectacular lack of resources, carrying out what he believed to be the clear will of God. "To open the way for this divine wish," he said once, ". . . God led me by the hand, quietly, little by little, until (his castle) was built . . . I have not had to calculate, as if I were playing chess; among other things because I have never pretended to guess the other person's moves so as to checkmate him later. What I have had to do is to let myself be led."

The young priest quickly attracted a group of university students, artists and tradesmen to his side and began to give them a Christian formation. He devoted his time especially to university students because he believed in the long term this would allow him to reach people from all walks of life. This pattern is still followed in Opus Dei when it begins to work in a new place. The founder worked tirelessly and Opus Dei gradually took shape. On February 14, 1930, only days after Monsignor Escrivá wrote that there would never be women members of Opus Dei, he said God showed him there would be women members.

It was not until 1933 that the first apostolic undertaking of Opus Dei began, despite great financial difficulties. Situated in a building on the corner of Luchana St and Juan de Austria St in Madrid, it was called the DYA Academy. The letters had a dual significance—they stood both for Derecho y Arquitectura (Law and Arquitectura) and for Dios y Audacia (God and Daring). Beside professional studies, this first centre offered cultural and religious training. There were spiritual retreats, talks, and meditations.

Not long after the DYA academy opened Don Josemaría began to attract opposition, often from within the Church. Outlandish rumours began to spread. Some people claimed Opus Dei members were nailing themselves to crosses. Some of the early claims have lasted to the present day. Others have appeared more recently. (An example was the claim in 1984 on a West German television station—Westdeutscher Rundfunk of Cologne (WDR)—that Opus Dei was dealing in arms. On that occasion Opus Dei sued.)

The difficulties caused by misunderstandings in the early years of Opus Dei were compounded by the Spanish Civil War. For periods of up to 18 months at a time Monsignor Escrivá was forced into hiding due to the severe religious persecutions which saw thousands of priests murdered. Several times he narrowly escaped the same fate.

Monsignor Escrivá had always lived personal poverty, making do with little in the way of clothing and food. He carried a workload that astonished those who came to know of it. But the rigours of wartime Spain began to take their toll. Don Josemaría lost weight and became incredibly thin. In the Autumn of 1937, when the dangers to his life became critical, the young priest, though he was ill, set out from Barcelona in the north-east of Spain on a courageous crossing of the Pyrenees to safety on the other side of Spain. The journey through rugged terrain and the cold and damp conditions lasted two weeks, with the hikers walking by night and hiding during the day. His companions said despite his condition Monsignor Escrivá spent most of his time trying to cheer them up. One of the men in the group, Antonio Dalmases, wrote in his diary: "The most moving moment of the trip was the holy Mass: a priest in our company says Mass on a rock. He doesn't say it like the priests in the churches. His clear and heartfelt words penetrate to our souls. I've never heard Mass like today. I don't know if it's because of the circumstances or because the celebrant is a saint. The communion is moving; we can barely move. We are dressed in rags, dirty and unshaven; our hair needs combing; our bodies, sleep; Our hands are bloodied with scratches, our eyes shine with tears; above all God is with us in the host."

Monsignor Escrivá's optimistic outlook was based on a deep confidence in St Paul's words: "all things work to the good for those who love God". He made it clear that anyone who lost sight of this basic spirit would not be doing Opus Dei: "Go about your professional duties for Love's sake," he counseled the members of Opus Dei. "Do everything for the sake of Love and precisely because you are in love. Even though you may taste the bitterness of misunderstanding, of injustice, of ingratitude and even of failure in men's eyes you will see the result in the wonders that your work produces . . ."

Early in 1939, after the war had ended, Don Josemaría returned to Madrid and started again. Before the war the DYA academy had already moved to larger premises in Ferraz St, Madrid, but everything was destroyed during the fighting. When he saw the rubble his efforts had been reduced to, Don Josemaría is said to have laughed out aloud, and renewed his faith in God's will. He spent the early 1940s re-establishing the work of Opus Dei and doing priestly work.

On February 14, 1943, the Sacerdotal Society of the Holy Cross was formed. The public criticism began again and did not abate, despite active support for Opus Dei by the bishop of Madrid, Don Leopoldo Eijo y Garay.

Nevertheless Opus Dei began to spread to other countries. In 1945 it went to Portugal, then to Italy, France and Ireland, the United States and Mexico, Chile and Argentina. In 1951 it reached Colombia and Venezuela, then Germany, Peru and

Guatemala, Ecuador, Uruguay and Switzerland. By 1957 it had spread to Brazil, Austria and Canada. Year by year it kept on expanding. In 1946 the founder moved to Rome partly to guide the long process of finding a suitable legal form for Opus Dei within the Church. Over the years the Popes appointed him to various posts. He was also appointed member of the Pontifical Academy of Theology, consultant to the Sacred Congregation for Seminaries, consultant to the Sacred Congregation for Catholic Education, and member of the Pontifical Commission for the Authentic Interpretation of the Code of Canon Law.

Meanwhile, Monsignor Escrivá travelled the world and spoke to large gatherings including members of Opus Dei, people who were receiving spiritual help from Opus Dei and others. He answered questions on diverse aspects of the spiritual life. On some occasions thousands came to listen— men and women, rich and poor, old and young. Films of these events reveal a lively man with great warmth and a sense of humour, whose comments go to the heart of a matter. Constantly he refers back to the need for love of God and man. His message is summed up in these words at a public meeting: "When a Christian carries out with love the most insignificant everyday action, that action overflows with the transcendence of God. That is why I have told you repeatedly, and hammered away once and again on the idea, that the Christian vocation consists in making heroic verse out of the prose of each day. Heaven and earth seem to merge . . . on the horizon. But where they really meet is in your hearts, when you sanctify your everyday lives."

The death of Monsignor Escrivá came suddenly. He suffered a heart attack on June 26, 1975, in his office in Rome before an image of the Virgin Mary. The loss was a great blow to the members of Opus Dei, but it did not appear to affect Opus Dei's growth. This was partly because Monsignor Escrivá had always emphasised that Opus Dei was God's work, not his. "You would have made a sorry bargain," he said, "if, instead of following Our Lord, you had come to follow this poor man."

In his later years he said: "Our Lord writes with a table leg and he writes marvellously, so that it can be seen that it is his doing, not the table leg's . . . I am nothing but a poor instrument, like a little donkey before God, a little donkey pulling the cart . . . For the greater part of these forty seven years, I have worked without enthusiasm, because the work had to be done; because God wanted it done and it was my duty to be his instrument: a bad one, but an instrument."

It is difficult to define what constitutes saintliness, but when you meet it you know it. It is like what the English writer Malcolm Muggeridge has written of Mother Teresa of Calcutta: "She has lived so closely with her Lord that the same enchantment clings about her that sent the crowds chasing after Him in Jerusalem and Galilee, and made His mere presence seem a harbinger of healing." The reaction of many when they have seen the founder of Opus Dei, even on film, has been similar to this. It has seemed to them that here is someone who emptied himself for something beyond the dimensions of this world.

One of the leading figures in modern psychology, the Jewish psychologist, Professor Viktor E. Frankl, once tried to define what was so attractive about the founder of Opus Dei: "If I am to say what it was that fascinated me particularly about his personality, it was above all the refreshing serenity which emanated from him and warmed the whole conversation. Next, the unbelievable rhythm with which his thoughts flowed, and finally his amazing capacity for getting into immediate contact with those he was speaking to." Professor Frankl added: "Monsignor Escrivá evidently lived totally in the present instant, he opened out to it completely, and gave himself entirely to it. In a word, for him the instant possessed all the qualities of the decisive."

Whatever his personal qualities, what attracted most people to Monsignor Escrivá was his preaching. It was clear, uncomplicated and above all, stayed close to the words of the Gospels. While he often illustrated points with stories and anecdotes, he always linked them in an immediate way to the teachings of Christ. Listening to him, there is no feeling of being carried along by human intellect alone, by the cleverness of a clever man. The same themes recur— awareness of being a son or daughter of God, detachment from the world, seeking and doing God's will and trusting in divine providence. All these themes were liberally laced with quotes from scripture; so much so that a critic of Opus Dei, an academic, once launched an attack on Monsignor Escrivá based partly on words he used in his homilies. The words were quotations from the Bible.

Monsignor Escrivá saw Opus Dei as part of the process which was bringing lay people to fully assume their responsibilities in the Church, and to participate in its mission in their own way. He believed a major part of Opus Dei's mission was to fight the idea that Christian life is something exclusively spiritual, proper to pure, extraordinary people, who remain aloof from the so-called "contemptible things of this world". He believed that when things were seen in this way, churches became the main setting for the Christian life and being a Christian meant going to church, taking part in sacred ceremonies, being taken up with ecclesiastical

50

matters, in a kind of segregated world, considered to be the ante-chamber of heaven, while the ordinary world followed its own separate path.

"The doctrine of Christianity and the life of grace would in this case, brush past the turbulent march of human history, without ever really meeting it," he warned. He argued that if the world had come from the hands of God, if He had created man to his image and likeness and instilled in him a spark of his own light, then the work of human intelligence must uncover the divine meaning in all things.

"No! We cannot lead a double life," he said. "We cannot be like schizophrenics, if we want to be Christians. There is just one life, made of flesh and spirit. And it is this life which has to become, in both soul and body, holy and filled with God. We discover the invisible God in the most visible and material things.

"There is no other way. Either we learn to find our Lord in ordinary, everyday life, or else we shall never find him. That is why I can tell you that our age needs to give back to matter and to the most trivial occurrences and situations their noble and original meaning. It needs to restore them to the service of the Kingdom of God, to spiritualise them, turning them into a means and an occasion for a continuous meeting with Jesus Christ."

At the time of Monsignor Escrivá's death Opus Dei had grown from a few university students in Spain to 60,000 members of 80 countries. As already pointed out, Monsignor Escrivá believed the creation of Opus Dei was the will of God. For Catholics, the contention is supported by the fact that the Church has officially embraced Opus Dei at every stage of its development. "With very great hope, the Church directs its attention and maternal care to Opus Dei, which—

by divine inspiration—the Servant of God, Josemaría Escrivá de Balaguer, founded in Madrid on October 2, 1928 . . . From its beginnings, this Institution has in fact striven, not only to illuminate with new lights the mission of the laity in the Church and in society, but also to put it into practise; it has also endeavored to put into practise the teaching of the universal call to sanctity, and to promote at all levels of society the sanctification of ordinary work, and by means of ordinary work.'' (Papal Bull 'Ut Sit', 28th Nov., 1982)

The process for Monsignor Escrivá's canonisation, supported by 69 cardinals and 1300 bishops, is continuing. During his life Monsignor Escrivá suffered a great amount of slander and discrimination. He always urged the members of Opus Dei to fight against this very human disease. Perhaps there is no better example of this than in Kenya.

4

KENYA
Fighting discrimination

IN 1958 racial tensions were running high in Kenya, a black African nation ruled by whites. The powder-keg atmosphere was made even more explosive because Africans were split into 40 separate tribes; some, long-standing enemies. A state of emergency was in force, the legacy of the Mau Mau rebellion which began in the early 1950s and took more than 10,000 lives, most of them black Africans; thousands more went to detention camps. In Nairobi most native Africans were servants; few were seen on the streets; none drove cars. In the classrooms of upper secondary schools there were no native Africans. But what the British Prime Minister, Harold Macmillan, would describe as "the winds of change" were already blowing fiercely in Africa.

"We came to Kenya with our project, the first multi-racial college in East Africa, something for all the races and for all religions," recalled Father Joseph Gabiola, Opus Dei's first priest in the country. "We feared the authorities would say: 'What do you mean? This cannot be. Are you mad?'"

The main obstacle was racism. Blocks of land in Nairobi, were generally for Europeans, Africans or Asians. Few could be used for the new college. The land, members of Opus Dei found, was in a European residential area and the neighbours objected. "Officially they objected because they did not want a school in the neighbourhood," Father Gabiola said. "But everybody knew the real reason was that the school would have black Africans. There was a meeting in one of the rooms of the local council and we had to go along to answer some questions. There was a huge crowd of whites outside and the thing became quite hot. I don't know why, but the whites were all abusing us. It was in all the newspapers, front page. And in the end they won. We lost the land."

As it turned out losing the first battle was providential. Another block of land was found in Strathmore Road (now Mzima Springs Rd). This time there was no room for complaint—it was adjacent to three European schools.

The goal was to build a boarding school which would bridge the gap between secondary and university. Previously native Kenyans had to leave the country to get a higher education. "There was a big gap there," Father Gabiola explained. "The aim was to create something to train the students in many areas: academic, human and, for those who wanted it, religious."

After the land problem came financial problems. The first principal, David Sperling, and teacher, Kevin O'Byrne, took the brave step of starting the main building before all the money was raised. The students were all poor so it was useless looking there for help. The colonial government gave some money, some was raised through mortgages, but it was not enough; so David Sperling set off for Europe and America in search of benefactors.

When the money problem was under control critics predicted the project would be a disaster anyway. A friend of Father Gabiola, a religious, warned him: "Its going to be a failure because you will not get the students."

"But," Father Gabiola said, "we were determined that, with the grace of God, it would work". David Sperling and Kevin O'Byrne travelled the country looking for students to put their faith in an institution that did not yet exist, and they were successful.

"When he heard of it, my friend said: 'Of course you will have Africans, but you will not have Europeans. And Asians, you will not have Asians.' Later I was able to tell him: 'We have found an Asian student.' His reaction was: 'Very good, very good, you will have one.' And then the Europeans wanted to come, through friendship because by this time we had many friends, and so it continued on."

In the early days conditions at Strathmore were primitive. The college was surrounded by bush which ran down into the Nairobi River valley. As students arrived all that could be seen over the maize in front of the new school was the boxes they carried on their heads. The land was infested with cobras. One day a leopard paid a visit, followed by a hyena which chased a student up one of the pillars at the entrance to the main building.

More formidable than the physical environment were the racial barriers. These were not restricted to differences between black and white: some tribes had less in common with each other than with the Europeans.

Father Gabiola remembered the scene on the first night: "They had told us the African students would be jumping through the windows, all kinds of things. We were full of wonder at what was going to happen. The first night I was out in the garden . . ." he opened his eyes wide in imitation of someone watching in anticipation and then broke into laughter: "But everything was silent. Everybody was studying."

Potential racial tensions were neutralised by Strathmore's family atmosphere, an approach inspired by the words of Opus Dei's founder: "We are brothers, children of the same Father, God. So there is only one colour, the colour of the children of God. And there is only one language, the language which speaks to the heart and to the mind, without the noise of words, making us know God and love one another."

The college shield carried three hearts and the motto was "ut omnes unum sint", may they all be one. In a homily at the first Mass at Strathmore on a temporary altar, Fr Gabiola first spoke of Strathmore as a family home. He remembered the surprise on the faces of students: "It was, I believe, a very bold thing to aim at, especially considering the large variety of races, tribes, nationalities and even religions, both among the students and the teachers. It could have been taken as a beautiful thought, as a figure of speech or as an empty dream, but it was taken in earnest, and all responded."

The response was seen in practical things. When one of the first students, Gabriel Mukele, arrived with only one set of clothes, the other students fitted him out with ties, socks and shirts and David Sperling donated his old school suit. Despite these gifts Gabriel felt he was too poor to continue.

He decided to drop out and take a job; but David Sperling talked him out of it; he arranged holiday jobs so Gabriel could earn enough to get by.

Integration influenced all aspects of college life. No room was occupied by students of a single race or region. The teachers' rooms were alongside students' rooms. Meals were served at tables of six: a teacher, a European and African students and so on.

One of the early residents, Jacob Kimengich, remembered: "At meal time I found myself sitting at the same table with the principal and, of course, the other teaching staff were also there; and we were eating the same food. This was drastically different from my boarding school days where the food and accommodation was not shared at all. In those days who could think of eating the same food with a Mzungu, let alone sitting at the same table and sharing the same residential building. It was totally unexpected."

Another early student, Wilfred Kiboro, reflected: "A tradition started in Strathmore from the very beginning that everyone's opinion, belief, custom, colour, creed was respected. We were taught to be mindful of one another and considerate. Students were encouraged to assist each other whenever possible. Hard work was a way of life.

"Another tradition I recall was respect for individual freedom. We had no written rules, no prefects or class monitors, no general supervised study. One was given the responsibility to exercise his individual freedom: to study in his own time, and to manage his life generally. I think this is one of the traditions that truly distinguishes Strathmore from similar institutions. It was in my two years there that I came to feel that I was really accountable for my actions, not because there were rules, but because a certain standard of excellence was expected of me. If I failed to achieve it, I could only blame myself.''

Even today Strathmore is believed to be the only institution in Kenya without prefects or written rules. The philosophy was spelt out to teachers at the school thus: "Show a man you trust him and sooner or later he will respond to that trust. Leave a person free to act and he will usually act in a responsible manner; if he does not act responsibly, then patiently show him how he was wrong and leave him free to act again."

Strathmore continued to break social conventions with Kenya's first interracial rugby team. The Africans had never played before because rugby was a white man's game; the new team did not go unnoticed. The first match was recorded in The East African Standard on June 8 under the headline: First Multi-racial Rugby Team Makes Debut; and in the Sunday Nation on June 11, 1961, under the headline: An Experiment on the Rugby Field. The news reached as far south as Johannesburg, with the Johannesburg Star carrying an action photograph of the Strathmore team entitled: Study in Black and White Rugby.

The experiment forced students at Strathmore to confront hidden prejudices. "The hooker in our team was white and the props were both big African fellows," Father Gabiola explained. "After the first training session, the hooker came and said: 'I don't want to play.' 'Why not?' I asked. He did not want to say, but eventually he whispered: 'I don't want to be with the Africans so close together.' Father Gabiola burst into laughter: "Well, it was there, the mentality was there. And it was something we had to overcome. And we did overcome it."

It was not long before 80 per cent of Strathmore's students

were being accepted at university. The college gained an international reputation, attracting students from all over English speaking Africa as well as from Rwanda and Zaire. It branched out, opening a school of accountancy in 1966, a lower secondary school in 1978 and a primary school in 1987.

Some current residents of Strathmore spoke about their experience. Matthew Ndegwa, who came to Strathmore in 1979, now works for the government as a civil engineer and is a co-operator of Opus Dei.

"Opus Dei taught me how to get my priorities right, to do first things first and to persevere with something to the very end, to carry out my duties," he said. "I am the first born son of a family of 12. In my country a first born son must give a good example for the others. He should also use his money to help the others, to help pay for the education of the younger ones which takes more than a third of my salary. The spiritual life Opus Dei introduced me to makes it easier to cope with the 24 hours of the day. It opens up my mind to my responsibilities and helps me not to ignore them."

Boniface Ngarachu, a teacher of accountancy at Strathmore, came there as a student in 1977. Already a Catholic when he arrived, he said he had learnt at Strathmore about the value of work, something he wanted to pass on to other people: "the idea that through work you can do something for your country, for your family, and your soul and that you can turn it into a prayer".

"There is also something else that has struck me," Boniface said. "Perhaps something that was very personal. I had many friends when I went to Strathmore, including girl friends, and when I talked to the priest I talked about them. Normally one shies away, but I felt I could tell him everything and I realised there was more in friendship. I realised there was something noble in it."

More than half the population of Kenya is Christian; about one third of them, Catholic. The population has been growing faster than any other country in the world, though only about 18 per cent of land is arable. Most native Kenyans still live on small farm settlements struggling to raise livestock and crops or working part time on the properties of wealthy landowners.

As you drive out of Nairobi you quickly come to tea and coffee plantations where native Africans labour all day under the sun to earn a modest wage. The women in particular have a hard lot. You see them struggling along the side of the road under huge loads. Further inland where the countryside is dryer, hotter, dustier, where the earth has to be worked hard before it will give even the most meagre returns, life is harder still. Many black Africans there live in thatched huts on bare earth floors as their people have done for centuries. They are nomads, continually migrating with their livestock and their few worldly possessions in search of grazing land and water.

For those who move to the city, it is a difficult transition. Regular work schedules, the faster pace and the impersonal way of life are difficult to adjust to. And there is the problem of the unequal sharing of wealth. The extent of this problem was brought home to me while travelling on a rattly old bus from the airport into Nairobi. It was not a bus that whites normally used. All the passengers were blacks.

From the bus you could see the shanty houses and claustrophobic housing developments where poor blacks lived. The little free land in these areas, including traffic islands, was used for shambas (the traditional Kenyan vegetable patch). The sea of faces waiting at each bus stop grew as you approached the city centre until there seemed to be hundreds of men, women and children trying to get on. It was a Saturday morning and on the footpaths you saw row after row of wretched stalls, sometimes consisting of as little as a few used vinyl belts on a piece of old cloth.

On the other side of town where the whites and wealthy blacks lived, things were different. The houses were impressive, even by the standards of developed countries. They were large and airy, the gardens pleasant, the driveways long and the hedges high. It is this contrast between rich and poor which Kenya must fight to overcome.

So far the country has managed to avoid the major political or social upheavals of other African nations; but there are no guarantees about the future. Security can only come with social justice and a national spirit which avoids large class distinctions. An essential part of social justice as it is promoted by Catholic moral teaching—and therefore by Opus Dei—is the free action of individuals. The Church's teaching recognises that good structures can never be enough to ensure social harmony and justice. No matter how good structures are, corrupt and selfish individuals can defeat them. On the other hand good citizens can succeed in making even a society with faulty structures work, the injustice of the system being counteracted by the spirit of individuals.

Over lunch in Nairobi I spoke with Wilson Kalunge, an assistant manager with an oil company and a member of Opus Dei. "One of the things which attracted me to Opus Dei was that here were people from other countries, but people who had a lot more concern for the development of this country than many of us. It was clear these people were the way they were because of the formation they had received. In Opus Dei I have learned that unless Kenyans become more concerned about the development of others some will end up wealthy while others among their countrymen are left far behind, struggling to survive. Either we accept our duties or we will end up with a classed society.''

Patrick Mwaniki, a maths and physics teacher at Strathmore College, told me before he met Opus Dei his goals were a high salary, a big house, a good car and a comfortable lifestyle. ''Now for me these are not the important things,'' he said. ''They are only means and not ends in themselves. In Opus Dei I have found your ambitions change to what you can do for people and society, not what you can do for yourself.'' Patrick said at school he had been involved in the Young Christian Association, debating and wild life societies and had ambitions of getting into politics. He said he found those ambitions fulfilled in the work he was now doing with youth. ''I feel I am having a real impact on society this way. Through the tutorial system at Strathmore you really get to know the students as individuals. I have had cases of boys labelled write-offs and in the space of two years I have seen at least three of these 'write offs' completely reformed. That is satisfying.''

Kianda Secretarial College, the first multi-racial educational centre for women in East Africa, is another project of members of Opus Dei in Nairobi. In the beginning there were only 17 students and they were all European. When the first application came from an Asian girl, the neighbours refused to consent. Again there was the problem of finding nonsegregated land. A site was eventually found on Waiyaki Way, 10 kilometres outside the centre of Nairobi, and Kianda became the first integrated secretarial college for women in the country. The fact was heavily publicised. One newspaper article said if anyone saw girls of different colours walking on the streets together they could be sure they were from Kianda College.

The often hostile reaction made life difficult; but racial discrimination was not the only pressure Kianda had to deal with; there was the question of sexual discrimination. In the early 1960s most African women, if they had jobs at all, had the worst; they were poorly paid; their living conditions and clothes were poor; the fees for a secretarial course were more than they could afford. Kianda was able to talk large firms into establishing a system of sponsorships. The new opportunity enabled the girls to find a career for themselves and to help support their often poverty-stricken families and clans. When independence came in 1963 Kianda was the only college training Africans.

Kianda has similar aims to Strathmore and has faced similar challenges. In 1966 it started a residential college for students who were new to Nairobi and had nowhere to stay. The more than 5000 students who have passed through came from all over East Africa, Ethiopia, Zambia, Sudan, Nigeria, Lesotho and Rwanda. Up to 17 nations have been represented at any one time, moving Kenya's Sunday Nation newspaper to comment in 1980: "Today the pan-African status of Kianda is a model for other African countries." In 1977 Kianda opened a high school. The Daily Nation noted in 1984 that the school took only seven years to become one of the nation's top 10 schools.

One goal of Kianda, as with Strathmore, has been to help

students overcome racial and tribal differences and to build strong characters. Students are encouraged to read widely and to improve their cultural background. Kianda's philosophy is that Kenya needs not only secretaries with fast shorthand and typing, but mature individuals with initiative, personality and responsibility. As a principal of the college, Miss Olga Marlin, described it: "people who can run an office, not just type letters." Some of the students have become teachers at the college. Others run businesses, such as data processing firms, shops and commercial farms.

Miss Marlin, who came to Nairobi to help establish Kianda in 1960, said Kianda did not stop at giving students a sound professional formation, but helped those who were practising Christians to improve their Christian life so that it permeated everything they did. "Monsignor Escrivá often warned against the danger of separating these two aspects," she said, "living a kind of double life, with God for Sundays and special occasions, on the one hand, one's professional and social life, on the other." Miss Marlin's successor, Miss Constance Gillian, outlined some of the qualities Kianda encouraged in its students as generosity, inner strength and calmness, tenacity and positive thinking.

Given the professional training that centres of Opus Dei like Kianda provide, it is clear that Opus Dei does not seek to restrict women to the home. Asked to comment on what a woman's mission should be Monsignor Escrivá once said he believed there need not be any conflict between family life and social life.

"I think if we systematically contrast work in the home with outside work," the founder of Opus Dei said, "retaining the old dichotomy which was formerly used to maintain that

Roberto Castellano, basketball coach at Centro ELIS, Rome, with some of his pupils.

Sports day at ELIS.

Students at the Seido School in Nagasaki, Japan.

The Saiki family, Nagasaki.

His holiness Pope John Paul II receives the Prelate of Opus Dei, Monsignor del Portillo.

Monsignor Escrivá

*His holiness Pope Paul VI greets
Monsignor Escrivá.*

*Kenya's President Moi greeted by Strathmore
College chaplain, Father Paul Mimbi, at the
college's 25th anniversary.*

The Ngigi family, Nairobi.

Assistant Town Clerk of Nairobi, Mrs Zipporah Wandera.

The Shrine of Our Lady of Torreciudad, in the Pyranees.

Judge Concha del Carmen, Madrid.

Stan Cosgrove, Dublin.

Madrid taxi driver, Joaquin Gracia.

a woman's place was in the home but switching the stress, it could easily lead, from the social point of view, to a greater mistake than that which we are trying to correct because it would be more serious if it led women to give up their work in the home.

"Even on the personal level one cannot flatly affirm that a woman has to achieve her perfection only outside the home, as if time spent on her family were time stolen from the development of her personality. The home—whatever its characteristics, because a single woman should also have a home—is a particularly suitable place for the growth of her personality. The attention she gives to her family will always be a woman's greatest dignity. In the care she takes of her husband and children or, to put it in more general terms, in her work of creating a warm and formative atmosphere around her, a woman fulfills the most indispensable part of her mission. And so it follows that she can achieve her personal perfection there.

"What I have just said does not go against her participating in other aspects of social life including politics. In these spheres, too, women can offer a valuable personal contribution, without neglecting their special feminine qualities. They will do this to the extent in which they are humanly and professionally equipped. Both family and society clearly need this special contribution, which is in no way secondary to that of men."

I asked several women in Kenya how Opus Dei had influenced their lives. One, Mrs Zipporah Wandera, had been an advocate of the High Court of Kenya. Her appointment as the first female Assistant Town Clerk of Nairobi created attention in the local press: in Africa women have generally been restricted in public life. Mrs Wandera, a convert to Catholicism and a member of Opus Dei, spoke in her office surrounded by books, papers and the offices of her male counterparts.

"In my job I have to deal with departmental heads and there are often difficulties," she said. "There are always politicians who are disgruntled because of the way you do things or because you do not want to do what they ask. African men tend to think very little of a woman's opinion. It is the way they are brought up. But the spiritual direction I have received gives me courage to stand up to people, even my bosses and if I think they are wrong I tell them.

"That is not to say that Opus Dei gets involved in my professional life. Opus Dei gives me spiritual formation and helps me to broaden my knowledge of Christian teaching but never tells me how I should solve any problem I have come across in my job. In fact, interference is something I have never heard of in Opus Dei and that is why I feel at home with it.

Mrs Irene Njai grew up in a rural area, but won a scholarship to study social work in Italy. She became a social worker, but when we met she was working as an airline ticketing officer because she said she could not bring herself to accept government policy promoting contraception.

"When I met up with Opus Dei I learnt about turning your work into prayer. I had been a Catholic so long, nobody had ever told me about this. I was told you should pray, but never that work could be turned into prayer; that you could say, I offer this work from eight to 10 o'clock to God for such and such a thing. I felt I was being guided in a special way. It was really very beautiful.

KENYA

"It isn't only the big things you can offer to God. When someone comes through the door at the office I think well here is a Son of God, there is a soul in this person and I try to help that person as best I can. Sometimes you will see a customer who looks very much irritated and tired and maybe frightened and you smile and you can change entirely the whole attitude of that person.

"Of course, we will never reach perfection, but little things pieced together produce something very nice. And I think this concept turns the day into something one looks forward to. To someone who has no concept of this, the day does not have this meaning. The day can be something that one dreads, as I used to dread it before. When one discovers that work is not a tragedy, it is a joy, it changes your life.

"Another thing I am grateful to Monsignor Escrivá for is this idea of marriage as a vocation. For example, his praise for human love. I have never heard it from anybody else. I had read quite a lot of books before I came to Opus Dei, but I never came across anybody who asserted marriage was a vocation as Monsignor Escrivá did. Nobody else has ever talked to me about this in the same way, showing me how to use the married life as the means for my salvation and my husband's salvation. And also there is the idea that we are the heart of the family and we need to be at the service of other people. As Monsignor Escrivá used to say: 'To put our hearts on the floor for the others to walk a bit more comfortably.'"

The house was tiny, made from bare boards, with a tin roof and a kerosene lamp for light. Mr Martin Ngigi and his wife, Jacinta, had invited me to dinner. Mr Ngigi is a traditional Kenyan farmer with a two-acre shamba. He had grown most of what we ate: chicken with a maize cake called ugali and a spinach-like vegetable called sukumawiki. Mrs Ngigi, a mother of six and a bank clerk, is a cooperator of Opus Dei.

"When I came across Opus Dei I had only two children and I had decided not to have any more," she told me. "But when I came into contact with Opus Dei I saw how good a Christian heart was in a big family. And I now have the four you see and I feel much happier since, so happy."

One of the younger boys, Josemaría, 9, took this opportunity to whisper to a friend who was with me that this was how he "came to be". "I was born in 1976," Josemaría confided. "That was the year after Monsignor Josemaría died."

Mrs Ngigi continued: "I used to think working at the bank was a terrible burden and the same with housework; but it is lighter now. These days I find it, well, a lot of fun."

Esther Lanoi Kuronoi, a member of Kenya's Masai tribe, famous for keeping old traditions, grazing cattle and living mainly on a diet of milk mixed with blood taken from cows. As a child she had wandered the dusty plains with the people of her tribe. Nevertheless she had enough schooling to become a student at the Kibondeni School of Institutional Management, a corporate work of Opus Dei which gives girls forced by poverty to drop out of school a chance to make a career for themselves; for some it is their only chance to break away from an environment where men have six to 12 wives and where women do most of the work.

At Kibondeni, Esther had been doing the two-year course leading to the National Certificate of Institutional Management which includes nutrition, dietetics, administration and accounts, nursing, languages and sociology. She had also taken classes in religious formation provided by Opus Dei: "I came to Kibondeni School two years ago," she said. "I had always been a Catholic, but here I learnt about how to keep to a spiritual plan of life and to sanctify my work: that is offering all of your work to God.

Esther said there was no tribalism at Kibondeni. The teachers emphasised that everyone was a child of God, no matter the colour of their skin or the tribe they came from. All the girls sat together with those of different tribes. One was from the Turkana tribe, a rival of the Masai. The two tribes had been fighting each other for a long time. At home, Esther said, she would never have been able even to talk to the other girl. "Here we tell jokes at get togethers about each other's tribes and everyone laughs," she said. "But we are good friends; when we leave the room, we leave holding hands . . ."

The experience in Kenya highlights something important about Opus Dei: why it can be controversial in some countries, but not in others. It is not because Opus Dei differs from country to country—it is always the same. The real reason is that standards of morality vary. Supporting equal rights for women in the 20th Century is bound to get you into trouble in countries where women are kept out of the workplace. But it will also attract opposition in those countries, some of them developed countries, in which women are denied the choice of being fulltime mothers and homemakers.

Opus Dei members went to Kenya when they did because they believed the time had come when they might be able to work there with people of all races, something Opus Dei has always insisted on. This is why Opus Dei is not yet in

South Africa. The apartheid policy there would require it to carry out its work separately with different races.

Despite the strong emphasis in Kenya on fighting discrimination, Opus Dei is not in any sense a single issue group. This was very clear in Spain.

5

SPAIN
A big spirit

IN the suburb of Vallecas, one of Madrid's most wretched quarters, where the founder of Opus Dei worked as a young priest, there is a school called Tajamar. As you enter the neighborhood you pass by a row of old cottages, black with age and neglect. They are much as they were 30 years ago when members of Opus Dei first came to the area. They reminded me of a Sydney slum where I used to go with my family to visit a dying aunt many years ago. Her neighborhood had cottages just like those in Vallecas. The misery they bred was revealed in the squalor and the bloody brawls which would often spill from them onto the street.

When Tajamar began in the late 1950s the poor of Vallecas had grown to expect outsiders wanted to take advantage of them. They had become hardened to politicians with empty promises and greeted the newcomers with contempt, hurling rocks and abuse at them. It took time, but the members of Opus Dei eventually succeeded in winning the confidence of locals and founded the school in an old stable. At first the local children would not come. The teachers walked the streets, found youngsters playing in the gutters and went with them to their parents to explain about the school.

At Tajamar, as in similar schools, they recognise that parents are the primary educators of their children. Each child has a personal tutor, someone they can talk to regularly about everything from studies to personal problems. Parents visit the schools regularly to speak with the tutor. The aim is to help each child grow academically, emotionally and spiritually.

In 1963 Tajamar started literacy and numeracy classes for parents. Some parents rose at 6 am, worked all day in a factory and then studied at Tajamar until 10 at night. Later, when unemployment became severe, Tajamar began technical courses in mechanics, electronics, printing, design and office administration. Today the primary and secondary school and polytechnic have about 2500 students between them. The government considers the school a model of its type and has sent overseas visitors there to see what is being done to educate the poor of Madrid.

My journey in Spain took in Madrid, Barcelona, the industrial centre of the north, Pamplona, the northern bull-fighting city made famous by Hemingway, and Torreciudad, Spain's famous shrine to Our Lady near the French border. Opus Dei is in many more cities, but even from the sample of its activities that follows, the diversity of people and projects is clear. More than anything else, Spain underlines the breadth of activities of Opus Dei's members.

One of the most visible signs of Opus Dei's presence in Spain is the string of schools members have initiated usually with others who are not members of Opus Dei. One of them, Pineda, is in a working class area of Barcelona, the northern zone of L'Hospitalet de Llobregat. It is an area where people cannot afford high school fees and parents have had to make great sacrifices. Though it started purely as a school for the young, Pineda has developed into a social support system. The area has problems with delinquency, prostitution and alcoholism, things for which most locals who are from small country villages are unprepared. One way the school helps is by counselling parents. The teachers said they normally advised parents not to react to the dangers in an extreme way, not to lock up their children, but instead to give them freedom while teaching them to use it responsibly.

This was an approach recommended by the founder of Opus Dei: "I always advise parents to try to be friends with their children," he once said. "The parental authority which the upbringing of children requires can be perfectly harmonised with friendship, which means putting themselves in some way on the same level as their children. Children—even those who seem intractable and unresponsive—always want this closeness, this fraternity, with their parents. It is a question of trust. Parents should bring up their children in an atmosphere of friendship, never giving the impression that they do not trust them. They should give them freedom and teach them how to use it with personal responsibility.

"It is better for parents to let themselves be fooled once in a while, because the trust they have shown will make the children themselves feel ashamed of having abused it—they will correct themselves. On the other hand, if they have no freedom, if they see that no one trusts them, they will always be inclined to deceive their parents."

The Writer

One afternoon at the historic Plaza Major in the old Madrid, the writer and journalist, Miguel Alvarez Morales, spoke to me over lunch about the impact Opus Dei had on his life. Miguel, an energetic man with a nicotine stained moustache, is the author of the historical novel, Alvar Nunez Cabeza De Vaca, about a Spanish adventurer shipwrecked off America. He has also published an account of the travels of Pope John Paul II, a book of history called The Post War Wars; and a collection of poetry, The Cane Flute.

"Every year I write an article to explain how I feel about Opus Dei," Miguel said. "It really changed my life. I always wanted a vocation but I was never meant to be a religious. I looked at all the orders, but I knew I wasn't being called to that. I loved the world very much. And then I met someone who spoke to me of Opus Dei. I said: 'One moment . . . what are you saying . . . that I can have my wife and poetry and . . . All the time I had felt God was saying to me: 'Come on, come on.' But I could not figure out what he wanted. Then it suddenly occured to me that this vocation to Opus Dei was what he wanted: to stay in the world but at the same time to be completely of God. To continue with my writing and my wife and children and still to serve God in everything."

So Miguel became a member of Opus Dei, stayed in the world and had a family of eight children. "I needed so many children to express myself," he laughed. "Every one has something, you know, and I needed all eight to express myself. It is like with God; there are so many people—Chinese, African, Spanish . . . He has so much to expressı One thing I love about the family is, like the Pope says, that the family is the only place you can be who you are. In the family you are just Miguel or Pepi or whatever. Everywhere in the world you are something: a poet or a journalist or whatever. But in the family you are plain Miguel."

The Taxi Driver

One man who came into contact with Opus Dei through sending his children to school at Tajamar, is Joaquin Puerto Gracia, a middle-aged taxi driver. A stocky, plain-speaking man with a ruddy complexion, he told me how he "did Opus Dei" in his cab: "One day a man got in the back and told me he had been drinking for four days. He had not been home to his wife and children and had spent most of his pay. When he asked me to have a drink with him I said yes, but instead of going to a bar I took him to a place where they had nothing stronger than hot chocolate.

"When he found out he could not get a drink he swore and told me to take off. He could not understand why I was interested in him. But when he settled down he began telling me about his life and I listened. When he finished I pointed to a church across the road. I said I was going there and asked if he wanted to come. Why, he wanted to know, should he want to go into a church when he had not been in one for years. But he came anyway. After a few minutes he said: 'You know, I feel good here.' Then after a while more he stood up and walked into the confessional. After that he stayed for Mass. The next day he rang me to say he had taken his youngest child to be baptised. We have been good friends for many years now. He doesn't go drinking any more and he is very good to his family.

The Housekeeper

Housekeeper and author, Marie-Therese Sanchez, appears regularly on television to talk about housekeeping. A member of Opus Dei for 36 years, she still had a great enthusiasm for her profession: 'I try to convert my work, the ironing, cooking, serving at table and making beds, into prayer, by doing things as well as possible and offering it to God," she said. "I try to find every day a different thing to improve in. I am convinced of what Monsignor Escrivá said, that work done well rapidly obtains good results in others. And a service to others is immediately a service to God."

Marie-Therese had been a successful student when she was younger and her teachers had told her she should study for a profession. They were amazed when she told them she believed housekeeping was the best profession of all. "As Monsignor Escrivá pointed out," she said, "it was the work the mother of God did and she was the most excellent of all creatures."

But many housewives were said to be unhappy? "Yes, it is true. But I would tell them the best way to avoid this is to always think of the others. It is true that housework is difficult, but it is also true that it has such good and immediate results."

The Glassblower

Enric Hernandez Sanchez, 58, a noticeably calm man with

a quiet voice and self-effacing manner, spends half of his life bent over a large wooden bench shaping glass over a burner. At first sight it looks a cosy life. He is his own employer and his creations—delicate roses, filigree vases, beautiful and glass bird cages—take your breath as they sparkle in the sun which streams into his workshop. But Enric had been a glassblower for almost half a century when he met Opus Dei and some of the sparkle had gone out of his work. Opus Dei, he said, made him aware of another dimension to his job.

"Before I met Opus Dei I was getting very old, not only in years but in a professional sense," he said. "I lacked ambition and enthusiasm for my work. When I met Opus Dei I experienced a rejuvenation. It made me realise work is a way to pray. I started to experiment, to try to design new things and I began again to get a great deal of satisfaction out of making beautiful things. And in the process I found out why I was a glass blower and not something else. I found there was a connection between my human vocation and my spiritual vocation.

"Before, I had felt a great frustration as if I had chosen the wrong profession. In the homilies of Monsignor Escrivá in Christ is Passing By there is the part about the parable of the sower. The seeds of wheat are scattered on the ground and there, where each of us falls, God wants us to give fruit. Wherever we are. This is where our daily struggle is.

"I supernaturalise my work first of all by offering it up to God. I try to do it the best I can. I am working always with material things and there is a lot that you can learn from matter, but, you should subject matter to yourself. So this is what I ask God, to be able to do things well, the best I can, so that they can be for his greater glory."

As well as primary and secondary schools, Opus Dei members in Spain have been responsible for a wide range of special purpose schools. Perhaps the most widespread are the agricultural schools or Escuelas Familiares Agrarias (EFAs) which cater for one of Spain's poorest classes: its farmers. At last count there were 36 EFAs carrying out more than 80 per cent of Spain's agricultural training.

Around 60 kilometres from Barcelona, in the Llucanes Hills I visited an EFA called La Casa de Quintanes. It was maintenance time at the old 17th Century building which has been converted into a home-away-from-home for 156 students. Blue-overalled students were running in all directions, wielding mops, repairing fences, driving a tractor. They were obviously enjoying themselves. The place had the atmosphere of a family home. On the lawn a couple of students wrestled with a dog, while the cook, who lives on the premises with her family, supervised some gardening.

The EFAs alternate formal classroom teaching with practical work on the farm. They also help farmers organise cooperatives to buy the latest farming technology, to commercialise their products and to protect the value of their goods and labour.

Another special purpose school, Brafa, is now one of Spain's most famous sporting centres. It began in 1949 when some members of Opus Dei played soccer with children in the back streets of a working class area of Barcelona and realised the area's need for organised sport. In the beginning they had no resources so they continued just as they had started: kicking a soccer ball in the streets and meeting in a borrowed garage. The existing complex of buildings and sports fields in the Artesania district was completed in 1971. Over 1700 boys and 500 men are now coached there.

Though it has produced national champions, Brafa's main aim is to get as many people as possible to participate in sport at their own level. Those who cannot pay are given scholarships. Apart from sports training the centre gives coaching in human virtues and cultural and spiritual formation.

A third special purpose school is La Veguilla, a centre for the handicapped just outside of Madrid. It consists of a primary and secondary school and a commercial workshop which allows those who have come from the school to use the skills they have learned to support themselves. The 90 men and women at the workshop spend their days creating ceramics, furniture and tapestries or cultivating plants. Their tapestries have been commissioned by the Lord Mayor of Madrid and the Queen of Spain. Those who administer La Veguilla said the workers found a new dignity and emotional stability simply by learning that they can be useful, that they can create practical objects and works of art that complete strangers are willing to buy.

Perhaps the best known educational venture of Opus Dei members in Spain is the University of Navarre in Pamplona. In Loves Labors Lost, Shakespeare wrote: "Navarre shall be the wonder of the world. Our court shall be a little academe, still and contemplative in living art." The people of northern Spain waited a long time for their little academe. It had been a dream held for centuries when the university of Navarre was founded in 1952. It came at a time when there was a critical need for institutions of higher learning in Spain and thus, like all the corporate works of Opus Dei, answered a real social need.

Leading professors came from universities around the

country, including Madrid, Barcelona, Seville, Santiago and Granada and from overseas. Many people branded the scheme as madness. The regional government had no confidence in it and a survey commissioned to gauge the prospects said it was impossible. When the news was broken to Monsignor Escrivá, he is said to have laughed and replied: "Of course it is impossible. And we are going to do it."

The first head of the university and later, President of the Friends of the University of Navarre, Professor Ismael Sanchez Bella, arrived by boat from Argentina where he had given up a chair in history. Excited, he asked the friends who invited him how much money they had collected. The answer took the edge off his excitement: "How much do you have in your pocket?"

Ismael told me: "We began without money, but with a lot of spirit which is more important than money."

Today the 250 acre campus has nine faculties. There are more than 10,000 students (500 of them from outside Spain) and 1000 professors. The emphasis is on "personalised tutoring" and ethical training. Classes in theology are also available. The government of Spain began recognising the university's degrees in the early 1960s. Navarre now has close contacts with other Spanish universities, including frequent interchanges and visits by professors and national congresses.

The policy at Navarre is to make higher education available to as many peole as possble regardless of their financial resources. The university gives financial aid to more students than any other university in the country. Over the years the institution has attracted little government funding. A large part in financing the project has been played by thousands of benefactors from all over Spain and overseas, many of whom have very limited financial means.

SPAIN

In many ways the heart of Navarre is its faculty of medicine which operates its own hospital. Notably, Navarre was the second hospital in Spain to perform heart transplants. But the Navarre hospital also stresses that medicine is not only to do with the pathology of the patient. It gives emphasis to spiritual care as well. Doctors and nurses at the hospital go out of their way to spend time not only with patients, but also with their relatives. On both days that I was there I noticed in the front foyer of the building a steady stream of doctors and nurses comforting visitors they had come to see off.

The other faculty I paid particular attention to during my visit to Navarre was the Faculty of Journalism which, when it began in 1958, was the fourth faculty in the university. Monsignor Escrivá is said to have urged it be established even though it was the first of its kind in Spain. At the time many prominent people said to treat journalism so seriously was "foolishness". Today the faculty is thriving, every year turning out hundreds of students who find employment in newspapers all over the country.

In an interview with a student journalist, the founder of Opus Dei once explained why he felt so strongly about journalism: "Journalism is a great thing, and so is university journalism. You can contribute a good deal to promote among your fellow students love for noble ideals and a desire to overcome personal egoisms. You can foster an awareness of social problems, you can encourage fraternity. And let me especially invite you to love the truth.

"I cannot hide from you that I am disgusted by the sensationalism of some journalists who write half truths. To inform the public is not to steer a middle course between truth and falsehood. That is not objective information, nor is it moral. People who mix in, together with a few half truths, a considerable number of errors and even premeditated slanders are unworthy of the name of journalists. They cannot be called journalists because they are only the more or less well greased tools of any organisation for propogating falsehood which knows that lies once put into circulation will be repeated ad nauseam, without bad faith, through the ignorance and credulity of many people. I must confess that as far as I am concerned false journalists come out winners, because not a day passes in which I don't pray earnestly for them, asking our Lord to enlighten their consciences."

In a book of this kind it is not possible to do justice to the magnificent work being done at Navarre by a small band of people with few resources. But the professionalism of the institution is indicated by the fact that links, such as the conferring of honorary degrees on professors, now exist with overseas universities such as the Sorbonne, Harvard, Coimbra, Munich and Louvain.

The different educational projects run by members of Opus Dei in Spain demonstrate the distinction between "personal" iniatitives and "corporate works" of Opus Dei. Whereas in the EFAs and La Veguila, Opus Dei does not take any responsibility (its members and the others who work there take full responsibilty) in the University of Navarre, in Tajamar and Brafa, Opus Dei has accepted the responsibilty for all doctrinal and spiritual formation.

The Farmer

Antonio Duran's face is red and lined, his hands rough and hard and his eyes set in a permanent squint from long hours in the sun; but you can see at a glance he is a happy man. He led the way through a maze of narrow little streets to his home, an old terrace house with the sweet smell of cooking and freshly harvested corn. While his wife prepared the evening meal, his children gathered around to listen to him explain how he made his living:

"I get up at 7.30 and work until 9.00 at night. I grow corn, olives and almonds, grapes and cereals and I make some wine. There is a lot of work and a lot of sacrifice. I try to do my best and to offer God my work. I have to run all the time but I try to take care of the details. God helps me. I have a crucifix on my tractor beside the wheel so I don't forget him."

Antonio paused to pour a glass of his home-made red wine and offer some of the almonds he grows. "I was brought to Opus Dei by an architect I met when he was working nearby. We were good friends and he brought me to a retreat. My wife is not a member but she goes to Opus Dei activities too. It is difficult life being a farmer with a family to support, but not too difficult. Everything is possible."

The Judge

Judge Concha del Carmen had been in Opus Dei for 20 years when we met. An attractive, well-groomed woman, she seemed light hearted, almost breezy, for a judge; there was none of the judicial gravity you normally associate with the bench. Relaxing in a comfortable chair, with rows of legal tomes on shelves behind her, she explained she was attracted to Opus Dei by the "human way of life, the family atmosphere, the gaiety": "It is very important for a judge to be very close to people and to go into their problems in real depth," she said. "It is something Monsignor Escrivá emphasises in one of the homilies in Christ is Passing By. Jesus Christ did many marvelous things for the poor and as a judge you come across society's most wretched individuals—the poor, the sick, the runaways. First you must work with the instruments that the law provides. It is difficult to do more because often it is hard to see the human side of these people. But Opus Dei has taught me many details of love, like paying attention to everyone and showing them respect. The easy way is just to get rid of them. The other way is to try to help them set their lives straight.

"But it is not only the big things that count. The little things are very important. For instance this afternoon I was hurrying my work. I had to write out a judgement to be typed out and when I finished I realised it would be difficult for the typist to read. So I wrote it out again, neatly. That is the kind of thing Monsignor Escrivá said was important—to do little things with perfection in order to grow closer to God and to help others around you."

A big Family

One Barcelona family well known to members of Opus Dei outside Spain is the Pich family. Mr and Mrs Pich are co-founders of a parents' education and help group which has spread around the world. The Pichs have also helped establish schools and youth clubs. They say their hobby is raising their 16 children.

Some people will frown on the idea of such a large family. But, while the late 20th Century has shown a preference for small families, many people are now beginning to question whether small is really beautiful. Recently the European

SPAIN

Community's Economic and Social Committee released a report showing the birth rate in EC countries had fallen to dangerous levels, well below the generation threshold—a major factor in what has become known as Eurosclerosis. "The demographic imbalance is reaching unprecedented proportions," the report said. "Making good the deficit in Europe would require immigration on a massive scale, unlike anything seen so far." Some governments, notably in France and Germany, have already reacted, offering financial incentives for couples to have children.

Mrs Pich was at a school meeting when I called at the Pich home. I spoke with Mr Pich while we waited. "The trouble with the way we tend to think about big families is we imagine the 16 enter through the door at the same time," he said. "It is not that way at all. They enter one after the other with about 12 months separating them. Now that is a key difference. Nature is very clever. Everything is very appropriately planned. So then, what is the difference between having six and seven children? Between the 10th and the 11th it is only 10 per cent and between the 15th and the 16th it is much less than that. So you see, when you look at the thing objectively there is no real problem." Mr Pich said up until the time when they had 12 children the family lived in a small flat with only three bedrooms for the children, but they were happy there and he wrote an article on how it was possible for a family of 14 to live in a flat. Now that they lived in a big house he said he could write a book on how you cannot live in a big house because you tend to lose people.

"One advantage of having a big family is that as the children grow up you find you have many little helpers," he said. "It can be shown with a bit of clever delegation the

85

parents of a big family have less work. Of course it is a task to organise a family but the answer is that you make it your hobby. And I can tell you it is more interesting, more amusing than 30 motion pictures. It is enthralling, fantastic!"

How was it possible to take care of the needs of many people growing up, all at different ages and stages of development? "Firstly you train the older ones well to act as the role model for the others. Who is the hero of a young boy? Always it is his older brother who is always bigger and stronger and more courageous and that is who he wants to be like. And for the girls, the older sister knows how to speak well, to dress and to be tidy. It is the same. A strong family atmosphere educates every member of the family, which means everybody participates in the education of the others. Everybody can help in their way.

"Even the little kids can do a great deal by being charming, by being very gentle, by doing a lot of little things. We can learn a lot from children if we just put up our antennas in an appropriate way, if we just listen to what they are saying and to what they want to say. This is something we can forget. We think we, mummy and daddy, are the key factor in educating our kids and while this is true up to a point, it is less than we imagine."

The conversation was interrupted by the evening meal which was taken around a huge circular table with large iron pots on a moving disk in the centre. During the meal Mrs Pich, a surprisingly youthful and serene looking woman, arrived to the cheers of the eight children still living at home. All joined in the conversation. Everyone had a story to tell about the day's events. When I asked what they liked most about being in a big family, they all burst into laughter. Rosa, the eldest, translated: "What we like most is that we are

always laughing. You see, we are all full of funny stories.''
They began to laugh again, slapping and falling against one
another and I began to feel as though I was in one of those
poor, but tremendously happy families that Charles Dickens
wrote about.

"There is an equation in a big family,'' Mr Pich reflected.
"The joys are all multiplied and the sadness is divided . . .''

After dinner and a family Rosary I asked Mrs Pich if perhaps
she had ever had yearnings to pursue a career outside the
home. She was nonplussed: "But I enjoy the work I do with
the children so much . . .'' she protested. She asked her
husband to tell the story about a woman he met in Chicago.
"She was a mother of eight children,'' he began. "A journalist
interviewed her and asked: 'But do you find yourself
realised?' This suggestion got the lady's back up and she
answered: 'Now wait a minute Mr newspaper journalist. I
am a lawyer. I worked before as a lawyer with my husband
and when the children arrived I decided to stay at home with
the children. Now with full respect for an office woman,
would you judge who is realising herself more, she or me?'
(Mr Pich demonstrated how the mother imitated a woman
sitting straight backed at a typewriter) '. . .eight hours a day,
or me surrounded by the personality development of all my
kids?'.''

Mrs Pich said her vocation to Opus Dei had helped her
through the difficult times, particularly the practice of setting
aside time each day to spend in quiet meditation. She said
it allowed her to recharge her batteries: "This is something
a housewife needs very much,'' she said. "And to see in all
the little things that happen in the family the presence of
God. This more than anything makes things run smoothly
and makes easy the things some people think are difficult.''

OPUS DEI

As you drive north from Barbastro, the silhouette of a large building comes into view against the sky in the rocky hills far away. As the road begins to wind you lose sight of the yellow and red brick church with its huge bell tower. Each time it reappears it reveals something more of its beauty. It is Torreciudad, a shrine to the Mother of God. Like other Marian shrines around the world, Torreciudad exists for one reason—to help the people who go there recover the spiritual direction of their lives.

The area around Torreciudad in the province of Huesca, less than 100 kilometres from the French border, was the site of the final Christian counter attack against the Moors in the 11th Century. Following the initial victories a shrine was built to honour the Mother of God. The 15th Century historian, Faci, recounts its history: "The holy statue takes its name from the place where its chapel is situated. It dates from the time of the reconquest of the district, in about 1083, by our King Don Sancho Ramirez. The Moorish garrison and inhabitants of the castle and village of Torreciudad having been driven out, the victorious Christians, dedicated the Mosque in honour of a holy statue of Our Lady which they had found nearby and which is the same one as is venerated today."

It was to this spot that Monsignor Escrivá's mother, like millions of people from all over the world, made a pilgrimage. It was 1904 and she covered the route to the shrine with her two-year-old son mounted on a mule. Mrs Escrivá had come to say thank you for the cure of Josemaría after doctors had given up hope of his recovery. In those days there was no modern road and the way was hard, particularly the last four miles which had to be covered on foot. Many mothers, and strong men as well, have come to give thanks for what they believed were similar favours.

Torreciudad, which looks down on the El Grado dam and is backed by the Pyrenees, has changed over the years. Thanks to donations from all over the world, a new shrine was opened on July 7, 1975. Inside, the focal point is a tableau, over 14 metres high, carved from 14 tonnes of alabaster and featuring the original image of Our Lady of Torreciudad. It depicts scenes from the life of the Mother of God—the betrothal, the annunciation, the visitation, the nativity, the flight into Egypt. But perhaps the most significant of all for members of Opus Dei is the image showing the workshop in Nazareth with Jesus helping St Joseph carve wood with an adze, as Mary, also working, looks on contemplating her son.

Under the main sanctuary is a crypt with three chapels dedicated to Our Lady of Guadalupe, Loreto and Pilar, and 40 confessionals. Monsignor Escrivá, whose promptings inspired the building of the new shrine, hoped that meditation there would lead many visitors to a renewal of their relationship with God. "What I hope for is spiritual fruit," he said, "graces which Our Lord will bestow on all those who come to venerate His Blessed Mother at this shrine. The miracles I would like to see are conversions and peace brought to many souls."

The founder of Opus Dei believed Torreciudad would show devotion to the Mother of God was not a thing of the past, that Christians were bound to love her "more than anything else on earth, after God; for above her there is none but God." His was the spirit of the Second Vatican Council which reminded all Catholics that "the cult, especially the liturgical cult, of the Blessed Virgin, be generously fostered".

Thus Torreciudad is a peaceful place of prayer. The quiet

and stillness is broken only by the pealing of a carillon of bells. Buses and cars are parked far away and signs request people to respect the atmosphere of Christian piety. There are no stalls selling cheap souvenirs and plastic images. On Sundays and on important feasts, particularly in May and October, the traditional months dedicated to the Mother of God, thousands of people, many of whom are not regular churchgoers, pour into Torreciudad. The shrine has been built for the service of the whole church and even on week days there are many visitors, particularly schoolchildren and religious.

In the old shrine there is a visitors' book which records the sentiments of those who come to visit. Some people still come for a favour: "So that the Virgin can give my father work. . .so that my family be like you. . .so that my girlfriend loves me." One was moved to poetry: ". . .more beautiful than the sun, that's how my mother is. . .". Another felt gratitude: "Thank you for the days we have passed here beside you. Help us so that we will be each day more Opus Dei." One man wrote simply: "Blessed Virgin, I love you."

It is said that in some Spanish cities there is a centre of Opus Dei on almost every street corner. While this chapter has offered little more than an introduction to the activities of members in Spain, it does indicate something of the range of areas they are involved in. It shows something of Opus Dei's ability to inspire people from all walks of life. Like the mustard seed in the Gospel, it has grown to be like a tree in which all the birds may find a home. Spain started me thinking more deeply about the breadth of Opus Dei's membership and works. But it was not until the end of the journey that its full significance became clear.

6

ENGLAND & IRELAND
A spirit that unites

ON a bus from Dublin airport the driver, a little smiling man, was running up and down helping people find their destination. As they were about to leave he would leap from his seat, dash down the aisle, help with their luggage and then turn away before they had time to think of a tip. I had not found service like this in any other country. Waiting at a traffic light he came to me and asked where he could let me off. My destination was Dartry Rd, not far from the city, and I had planned to catch a taxi there. "Ah, it wouldn't be a cab you'd be wanting," he protested, returning to the wheel. "No, you don't want to go wastin' y' money on a cab when there is another bus that would be takin' you there just as well." Soon after, we came to a halt and he reappeared. Handing me my luggage he advised: "Now just fetch y'self across the road there to that bus stop and you'll be getting a number 14 bus to take y' right to y' man's door.

Ireland has a special place in the English speaking world. She is celebrated for her charm, her music, her legends, but most of all for her people. Her magnetism is reflected by the number of Americans claiming Irish ancestry—around twice the number who could possibly qualify. You find the same thing in Australia.

The attitude to Ireland in England is different. Historical conflicts have emphasised the lack of unity between the two countries. These days the divisions between the people of England and the Republic of Ireland are more apparent than real, but they are there. While, as the last chapter shows, the spirit of Opus Dei encourages diversity, it also encourages unity. There seemed to be no greater evidence of this spirit of unity than in England and Ireland; the essence of it was an attitude to service.

The need for spirit of service comes through many times in the Gospels. Christ made it clear that serving others was necessary for unity. This truth is underlined in the book, Illustrissimi, a collection of letters by the Patriarch of Venice, Cardinal Albino Luciani, before he become Pope John Paul I. In one letter, Cardinal Luciani tells a fable about a Korean general who dies and is taken to heaven, but allowed to see hell first. Hell, he finds, is an enormous hall with people seated around long tables with bowls of rice and very long chopsticks, too long in fact to eat with. The result is a room of frustrated people going through excruciating agony trying to feed themselves. This was their torment, this was hell. The scene in heaven was remarkably similar—again there were people with bowls of rice and long chopsticks, but this time they were perfectly happy and united, for each one was using the chopsticks to feed the person opposite.

The founder of Opus Dei once said. "I really wish we Christians knew how to serve, for only by serving can we know and love Christ and make him known and loved . . . If we are to serve others for Christ's sake, we need to be very human. If our life is less than human, God will not build anything on it for he normally does not build on disorder, selfishness or emptiness. We have to understand everyone; we must live peacefully with everyone; we must forgive everyone."

In England and Ireland many members of Opus Dei from all walks of life spoke about the spirit of service . . .

Over lunch in one of the oldest family hotels in Dublin, Buswell's, proprieter Noel Duff explained that for him service meant making sure those who came to his hotel had everything they needed and were made to feel at home. "I get together with the staff every week to discuss these things, to make them more aware of them," he said. "I even tell those who are interested what I know about sanctifying work. I know some people would say: 'You are an innkeeper, it is your job to give service, that's how you make your money.' But you see there is a key difference—it's not in order to make money that the concern comes in. And the service is not restricted to material things; it is a matter of taking an interest in each person and not being too rushed with them. Before I met Opus Dei I certainly would not hesitate to let people know I was terribly busy. Now I have learnt to make time; I don't let them know there is something else I could be doing."

OPUS DEI

Stan Cosgrove, a middle-aged vet who is a leading authority on racehorses, travels the world to work for leading trainers like Robert Sangster and Australian trainer, Tommy Smith. A knockabout fellow who likes a Guinness, he said the emphasis on service was a new thing for him. "It has given me a much broader view of things," he said. "We were brought up in our age with a concentration on the 6th and 9th commandments. We thought once we mastered the 6th and 9th wings were starting to sprout out of us, but we didn't even consider all the faults of pride and laziness. They didn't count at all once you got the 6th and 9th right.

"And then you had the opposite extreme, like the missions we used to have at my old parish. I remember one where the priest came along, a real thunderer, and he told us: "Everyone in this parish is damned". A fellow down the back began to laugh. So the priest called out: "And what are you smiling about?". The fellow looked up at him and said: "I don't belong to this parish."

"But on a more serious note, those missions could be very tough going. Everyone was damned and people got terrible guilt complexes and in our age a lot of them were affected. We never heard much about love. For me, Opus Dei changed that; it gave me a broader view. I would say before I came to Opus Dei I was moving towards complete self sufficiency. It was something I had been aiming at, a real goal in my life: not to have to rely on anyone but myself. These days I see that sort of thing as the lowest form of life. I mean that attitude is like the Pharisees. Opus Dei has changed all that and shown me that we all need each other."

Henry Kobis, had been a London perfumer for 37 years of his professional life, developing new scents to go with everything from washing powders to the creations of high class fashion designers like Mary Quant. Creating fragrances is an intense occupation, one which has been compared to composing classical music. But Henry said for him a perfumer's attitude—the desire to give others pleasure—was more important than technical expertise. This was something he tried to impress on young perfumers that they needed to have love for their work. "I tell them that unless they put their heart into it, the perfume will always be incomplete," he said.

For Henry, part of the spirit of service was being a good listener. In his job he talked to many people—executives of his company, fashion designers and so on: "In Opus Dei one thing you learn is to be sincere," he said. "With most people you would expect them to clam up. But when you show them sincerity they shed their facades. They open up. One thing I have discovered is people are dreadfully lonely, even the successful people, and this is because they are afraid to be themselves and are playing up to a facade. They have not found anyone who is sincere. Even if they earn good money, and have an expensive house and car there is still this dissatisfaction with themselves. It is a great help to people if you don't show them a facade. Instead you show your shortcomings and they appreciate that and they open up.

"Another thing I have found is everybody has some supernatural yearning, even the most crafty businessman. There was a technical director once who was disliked by everybody. They all thought he had absolutely no softness or sentimentality in him. After several months he admitted to me he was frightened. He was not sure of himself. So I told him to rely on the Almighty and tell him about his problem. He took the advice and people started to see a difference. He softened."

Geraldine O'Connor, a Dublin radiographer came into contact with Opus Dei while studying in England. A cheerful woman with an Irish love for telling stories, she spoke of some of her experiences visiting the old, the sick and the lonely with well-to-do friends who would normally never venture into the houses of the poor; many, she said, took as much from the experience as those they visited. "I have one friend, a Belgian girl, who came with me to see an old man living in a very run-down place," Geraldine said. "He was trying to light the fire when we arrived, so we lit it for him. We were eating some biscuits when there was some noise in the background and he said in a strange voice: 'They are coming again.' His eyes widened a little. I didn't know what he meant. I thought he meant people were coming from the hospital or something. 'They' turned out to be rats. As we sat at the table one jumped right across us. I couldn't take it. I ran out. But my friend stayed. And afterwards I could see there was a change in her. I am convinced there is grace in these incidents."

There were more stories of visits to the poor at Dublin's Anchor Club, a club for boys in the middle of an industrial housing estate with a reputation for broken homes and adolescent problems. The club helps the youths of the area to use their spare time well through courses in mechanics which involve building, repairing and riding go-carts and bikes. Jimmy Murray, a fitter and turner who works at the club, spoke of a visit he made with a young friend from the club named Eddie. The two of them went to see an old man living on his own following the death of his wife. Previously he had been a fine gardener but had let it all go; he had lost hope after some local kids smashed up his glass house. So Jimmy brought Eddie to see him and Eddie kept asking questions about the old man's life. Jimmy had told Eddie about how the garden used to be and he asked for a look. "The expression on that guy's face when he saw what these lads had done to that garden," Jimmy said. "It went in very deep with him."

Eddie went home that evening and two days later his mother rang Jimmy and said: "Where did you take that fellow the other night? He hasn't spoken a word for two days. He is going around in a daydream here." So Jimmy went to see Eddie.

"He was all tensed up about the old man," he said, "trying to work out what he was going to do about it. So Eddie goes down to your man's house and announces to him: 'I want to look after your garden'." The old man agreed. Eddie started to work in the garden. Then he saw the kids who did the damage playing nearby and he went after them. He brought them in and explained what they had done. "The next thing I heard," said Jimmy, "these kids were working in your man's garden. Before you knew it the old man was out there himself again. The incident changed the old man and it changed Eddie too."

In England and Ireland the members of Opus Dei have made the spirit of service a basic foundation of the social works they have initiated. In 1952 Opus Dei had been in England barely five years, the first members were students, finance was short and the idea of starting a student residence was an ambitious one. It was the hard work and sacrifice of many people, including non-Catholics which created

Netherhall House, a student residence in London's Hampstead Borough which has since been a home for students from 100 nations.

When the Queen Mother, Queen Elizabeth, opened a new section of Netherhall in 1966, she said it was important to have a home "from which have grown the beliefs and standards which remain throughout one's life", and added "I cannot imagine a better place to foster such standards than Netherhall House, which is based on Christian traditions—above all the tradition of service."

Like its sister institutions, Grandpont House and Greygarth Hall at Oxford University and in Manchester, Netherhall encourages students to treat study as a serious obligation. But it also encourages them to be outgoing and to help others—an ideal summed up by a tapestry in Netherhall's main living room which says: "a brother helped by his brother is as strong as a walled city."

Netherhall promotes the idea that professional work can be a service, even when a person earns their living from it. The idea was taken up in Netherhall's 25th anniversary magazine which explained the founder of Opus Dei wanted centres like Netherhall to spread the spirit of service by example. Some of the results, were visible: boys clubs like the Netherhall Boys Club, Kelston Club in South London. But others were less tangible. They were expressed through former students who had gone abroad to countries like Kenya, Nigeria, Japan, Malaysia and the Philippines, with the idea of serving others; they included everyone from a Kenyan eye specialist to a Russian scientist who was an atheist.

On the banks of the Thames near the former home of St

Thomas Moore, is Dawliffe Hall, a student residence. It is also the home of one of London's more successful girl's clubs, the Tamezin club, a non-denominational project with 180 members offering tuition in music, sports, dance and drama. Of it, an article in the London Daily Telegraph once said: "it is difficult not to make the club sound rather too good to be true . . ."

Two of the women who run Tamezin, Eileen Cole and Margaret McCreadie, explained it tried to give stability to young girls, particularly to those who came from the area's many broken homes. "When they reach their teens most of the girls wander off, but many come back," Eileen said. We try to give them the formation to grow up to be good mothers of families, responsible adults, and to be able to work well."

Tamezin club members run a similar project in Brixton, one of London's poorer quarters known around the world for the race riots which have occured there. Even in periods of calm, it is still a rough area. Margaret spoke of her first visit there: "I took a girlfriend with me. We were just walking out of the tube and I was telling her how the area had the highest crime rate in London when a fellow appeared and robbed us.

"There were problems at the club in the beginning too. Some of the children were pickpockets. It's a kind of sport with some of them. There is a lot of hardship in the area and until the children get to know what the club is about these things happen."

Before leaving Dawliffe Hall, I spoke to housekeeper, Lynn Hinge, about her attitude to spirit of service: "The way I look at it, I am a mother of a family," she said. "It is a bit large for a family, but you treat them in the same way as any other family. You look after them. If someone is not well and you know there is something special they like, you prepare it for them to make them feel better. Or with the laundry, the cleaning or the meals. You know that one likes it this way, one that way and you try to give them what they want. If someone sends down their clothes for washing and there is a tear, well you could send it back that way, but you don't, you repair it because you want to love those people through that work. People who come here and see this place tidy and clean know straight away it is a family. You know, the family is the foundation of society. It is not surprising that things go bad when the family is not what it should be."

In Ipswich, England a small group of Opus Dei members had started a parent-run boy's club. The founders, film director, John Pitt and Dr Tom Ward, succeeded in getting veteran film actor Sir Alec Guinness, to become patron. The club was financed through jumble sales and week-end buying and selling ventures. A local Congregational minister and his parishioners helped. Tom contacted several charities. One wrote back and asked sceptically: "How do you give moral formation in this day and age? It's not possible." Tom phoned the man, explained the venture and when he continued to doubt advised him not to worry so much about the money, but to pray. "Soon after I got a cheque in the mail for 10,000 pounds," Tom said. "I had to count the zeros several times before I could believe it. Underneath was written: The Power of Prayer."

The club has courses in film making, computer studies, archery, sailing, canoeing and wind surfing. Tom described it as an attempt to supply an "adolescent raft to independence". "As Monsignor Escrivá said, what we laymen have to do is stand on our own feet. If we place our responsibilities on someone else, on the hierarchy of the Church or any other organisation, if we abdicate our responsibility, it won't work."

After a guided tour of the club premises, John Pitt took me home to meet his wife, Joanna, and their children. Over dinner John and Joanna explained that in the beginning they had been wary about Opus Dei. Their suspicions were aroused by an article in The Times newspaper which painted an image of Opus Dei as some kind of excessive fringe group within the Church. Their son, Guy, had become involved with Opus Dei and they were both worried. So John investigated; he was determined, he said, not to let Guy go without a fight. He began to follow him. He even started going to Opus Dei activities. The result was he became a member himself.

In Opus Dei there is a strong link between the emphasis on spirit of service and trying to do all things well. The founder of Opus Dei emphasised that Christ called his followers not so much to be poor, but poor in spirit. This meant being detached from material possessions so that you could give the best you have to God and the service of others. This approach was demonstrated nowhere more than at Dublin's Cleraun Study Centre, the first centre of Opus Dei in Ireland to be built for the purpose from the ground up. Though the people who built Cleraun had no money to spare they insisted on doing things well, using quality fittings, carpet and wall hangings. Some of the extras originally planned for the building had been sacrificed in order not to settle for anything less than quality.

Monsignor Escrivá once illustrated the spirit of poverty and detachment in the following way: "As far as I am concerned, one of the signs that we're aware of being lords of the earth and God's faithful administrators is the care we take of the things we use; keeping them in good condition, making them last and getting the best out of them so that they serve their purpose for as long a time as possible and don't go to waste. In the centres of Opus Dei you will find the decoration simple, attractive and, above all, clean, because poverty in a home is not to be confused with bad taste or with dirt. Nevertheless, it seems quite natural to me that, in keeping with your means and your social and family commitments, you should possess some objects of value which you take care of with a spirit of mortification and detachment.

"Many years ago, 25 and more, I used to visit an eating place run by a charitable group for the benefit of beggars who were so poor that their only food each day was the meal they were given there. There was a large canteen looked after by a number of kind women. After the first meal was served, more beggars would come in to finish off the left overs. Among this second group of beggars one man in particular attracted my attention. He was the proud owner of . . . a pewter spoon! He would take it carefully out of his pocket, look at it covetously and, after he had downed his meagre ration, he would look at the spoon again with eyes that seemed to exclaim: 'It's mine!' Next he would lick it a couple of times to clean it and then, with deep satisfaction, would hide it away again in the folds of his coat! Here was a wretchedly poor beggar who, among his companions in misfortune, thought himself to be rich.

"Around that same time I knew a titled lady who belonged to the Spanish aristocracy. In the eyes of God such a thing counts for nothing. We are all equal, all of us are children of Adam and Eve, weak creatures with virtues and defects, and capable all of us, if Our Lord abandons us, of committing the worst crimes imaginable. Ever since Christ redeemed us there are no distinctions of race, language, colour, birth, or wealth: we are all children of God. This lady of whom I have just been speaking lived in an ancestral mansion. But she spent next to nothing on herself. On the other hand she paid her servants very well and gave the rest of her money to the needy, while depriving herself of almost everything. This lady had many of the goods which so many people are anxious to obtain but she personally was poor, given to mortification and completely detached from everything. Am I making myself clear? In any event, all we need do is listen to the words of Our Lord: 'Blessed are the poor in spirit, for theirs is the Kingdom of Heaven.'

"If you want to achieve this spirit, I would advise you to be sparing with yourself while being very generous towards others. Avoid unnecessary expenditure on luxuries and comforts, whether out of caprice, or vanity, and so on. Don't create needs for yourself. In other words, learn from St Paul to live in poverty and to live in abundance, to be filled and to be hungry, to live in plenty and to live in want; I can do all things in him who comforts me'. Like the Apostle, we too will come out winners in this spiritual combat if we keep our hearts unattached and free from ties."

The founder of Opus Dei believed this spirit of poverty, together with spirit of service could play an important part in uniting people, not only in England and Ireland, but everywhere. Both things are integral to the spirit promoted by Opus Dei in all countries. According to that spirit, service is something which should inform everything, even the smallest everyday activities. One of its most obvious expressions is Opus Dei's work with the poor.

7

MEXICO
Working with the rural poor

FOR mile after mile as you travel south of Mexico City in the state of Morelos the sun beats down on bleached and dusty fields, tired from centuries of squeezing out beans and corn. Shabbily dressed peasants in faded cotton pass by under large loads or balancing on the flanks of donkeys. The fierce heat is wasted here; there is little moisture to be sucked out of the earth. But as you come to an ancient hacienda near the little town of Chalcantzingo the fields are green; the landscape comes alive. The huge dome and towers of an old church look down on a small colony of buildings with whitewashed walls, red bricks and tiles. Under a huge tree at the entrance to the hacienda an Indian woman and her young son are retrieving fruit with a long pole. This is Montefalco, a centre where members of Opus Dei are working with the rural poor.

Originally a prosperous sugar business, Montefalco was burnt to the ground during the revolution of 1910 by the troops of Emiliano Zapata. Local members of Opus Dei joke that Zapata was the first Mexican co-operator of Opus Dei: thanks to him the modern owners gave the hacienda's ruins to them in 1949.

In the beginning the gift was more of a liability than an asset. The buildings were crumbling and infested with jungle and the local Indians, the Campesinos, were wretchedly poor. But, after years of work by many volunteers Montefalco is a place of beauty, a rich contrast of colors and textures, of old and new. The main square, the size of a football field, is surrounded by two retreat houses, the old church, a guest house and two schools.

The second challenge at Montefalco—helping the area's impoverished peasants—was as demanding as the building renovataions. When Montefalco was a sugar business, canals brought water from the snow caps of the Popocatepelt volcano. But a town up stream decided it had a greater need for the water and cut the flow to the Amilpas Valley. Why did the people of the Amilpas not do something? "We did," a campesino explained, "we complained. And when we complained they gave us a choice. They said: 'Do you want water or do you want bullets?' The other town was a big town with many bullets . . ." The only supply of water left to the farmers around Montefalco was a short, four-month wet season.

Thus the Amilpas valley became one of the most crime ridden in all of Mexico. During the long eight-month dry season the men spent too much time riding bulls and drinking tequila, and many family feuds broke out.

But there was another side of the people of the Amilpas Valley—the strong faith which helped many survive the poverty around them. One of the priests at Montefalco, Father Jose Adolfo Martinez, told a story of an incident that happened soon after he arrived in the early 1960s. The villagers had come and asked him to lead a procession to pray for rain. It was the wet season, but it had not rained for three months. They had with them what they called "the cross of the old lady", a huge image of the crucified Christ. Father Martinez reluctantly agreed to go along, but warned if God did not want it to rain it would not rain. "No father," the Indians protested. "If we do the pilgrimage it will rain."

Father Martinez said he felt foolish leading a ragged band of pilgrims through the parched streets under a cloudless blue sky, each covered by sheets of plastic in readiness for the expected rains. A non-believer sitting on his front door step as they passed broke into laughter and called out: "Whatever water falls, I will drink it."

"Of course, no sooner was the procession finished when it came down in buckets," Father Jose said. "It was the kind of praying that frightens you." On the way back to town, as they were passing the house of their sceptical friend, the pilgrims called to him with great satisfaction in the pouring rain: "Drink it! Drink it!"

When Opus Dei members first moved into Montefalco the local campesinos were suspicious. But some farmers became curious about the crops being grown there. A few accepted an invitation to study agricultural techniques. Thus, El Penon, now a full secondary school with an emphasis on modern agriculture, was launched with a modest class of five students. At El Penon they taught the locals practical things like the use of fertilizer and how to make the most of the rain before the dry season set in; even how to write their names. The campesinos had only two crops: corn and beans. At El Penon they taught them to grow tomatoes, onions and carrots and they taught the local people how to eat them so there would be a market. Then came lessons in raising chickens and pigs and instruction in how to start up a cooperative for buying and selling.

One farmer who lives near Montefalco, Juan Garcia, used to produce a meagre annual crop of beans and corn. In 1969, after his son had been to Montefalco, he began poultry farming with 3000 chickens a year. Juan, dressed in clean new overalls, showed me his poultry sheds which now turn out about half a million chickens a year. "That is how we can afford the truck and the running water and the bathroom," he explained.

Between 1961 and 1965, 40 students passed through El Penon. In 1971 the secondary school was started. In 1965 they began a 3-year diploma course. In 1971 the governor of the state paid a visit, was impressed and initiated a joint course on livestock. Today El Penon is one of Mexico's leading TV secondary schools, a school which combines live teaching with educational programmes on television. A girls' school, started in 1959 with classes in home economics, has introduced the local women to dressmaking, new cooking techniques, ironing, modern dressmaking, hygiene and the principles of good diet. Some of its former students have established a clothing factory which supplies retail outlets in Mexico City.

One farmer, Miguel Angel Senedo, who was married with three children, finished his studies at El Penon in 1974. With his father and brother, he had started to raise livestock, chickens and pigs, grew peanuts and tomatoes, and had replaced his oxen and donkey with a tractor. We chatted in his modern grain shed. Next to the crop dusters hanging on the walls and the radio playing pop music was a framed picture of the Sacred Heart. Miguel said life was good now but a few years before his family had problems. His father, a heavy drinker, became sick. The family was falling apart. No-one talked. But things began to change when Miguel started to put into practice what he had learnt at El Penon about raising chickens, pigs and crops. The family began to work together and his father joined in too; he began to reduce his drinking and eventually cut it out altogether.

"At El Penon I also learnt about spiritual things," Miguel said. "I try to live the way they taught me. When I work I tell God it is for him. When I sow my crops for instance. Just now I received some new chicks to be fattened and I offered the work I would do with them to God and I asked God that all would go well. Sometimes your mind wanders away from God for a long time, maybe for a whole day, especially when everything is going well or when you get tired of work. Sometimes I get lazy and say to myself: 'From now on I am not going to work hard. I am going to take it easy.' But then God sends you a problem and that sort of makes you come back to him and say: 'don't forget me'.

"Some days I get very tired from my work and I come home and I don't want to talk to anyone. But then the next day I start to try again and I ask God for help. At Montefalco they spoke of struggle for the sake of the others and that is what I try to do."

Marcos Torres is a member of Opus Dei, a farmer who raises crops and breeds chickens in the town of Jonacatepec. It was dusk and the front door of his house was open. As he spoke children played outside and tractors rumbled in the narrow street on their way back from the fields. He said Opus Dei had taught him that apostolate meant being a good friend. You had to start with people from the bottom, he said; not the ones who went to mass on Sundays, but the kind who got paid on Saturday and afterwards went to the canteena and spent all their money on tequila. "Some of my friends spend all their money there," Marcos said. "After they have done it many times they lose their shame, even if it means they have to go to a friend and ask for money to feed their children. Sometimes they just go out to someone else's land in the night and take what they need. They know the other man has worked hard to grow the food, but they do it anyway."

Marcos said he had a friend with this problem, as well as a problem with women. He came from a Catholic family, but they had never lived their religion. His father, taught him to gamble on cock fights, to ride bulls and to go to the canteena. "This man has had two illegitimate children," Marcos said. "But he is still a good man. He is a farmer and he has been responsible in his work. And I think he has begun to straighten out his life. You see he used to speak about his problems. I used to go to the bull fights with him and have a drink with him but I never got drunk. He knew that I lived a clean life and did not have a lover. After a while he asked me how I could drink but not take enough to get drunk. I told him it was not so hard when you tried. He is a man who loves his daughters and he wants them to have good life. So I asked him once if he continued to live the way he was how could he give his daughters advice about how they should live. I did not preach to him; I told him things slowly, over a long time. Now he has quit drinking and there are no more women. He is closer to his wife and sometimes he goes to Mass."

Margarita Barranco lives near Montefalco in the town of Chalcantzingo. Her home consists of one room separated by a curtain, a bamboo wash house and a small enclosure for cooking tortillas. She was widowed early in her married life when her husband was shot dead just outside a little stone church opposite their house. The murderers had mistaken him for another man. So Margarita was left to raise three girls and a boy, all under six years of age. To support them she raised some pigs and chickens, made clothes and baked tortillas and worked part-time at Montefalco. At Montefalco, she said, they taught her "how to take care of the vegetables, how to take care of the cows and how to take care of the children".

"I tried to teach the children about the important things first by living them myself, things like going to Mass," she said. "I tried to teach them how to be organised and how to treat other people. I taught them what they said at Montefalco: to be happy even though you have problems. And to help people live who don't have enough money. When I wake up I offer the day to God and during the day I offer all the things that are difficult. I offer the things that maybe other people don't think are important, things like keeping each thing in its place."

After the death of Margarita's husband some of his relatives collected a large sum of money to hire a gunman to track down his killers. It is the usual thing in the Amilpas Valley. When she heard of it Margarita went to her relatives and pleaded with them not to take revenge.

"But we have already paid our money," argued the

relatives. "We cannot get it back." "Then you will have to lose your money," Margarita replied.

A friend who told me the story commented: "She is such a meek little woman, but on this occasion she made a firm stand."

Bernardo Heredia had been going to Montefalco for several years. He was well-off by local standards, employing 20 workers on his farm, but before he came into contact with Opus Dei he thought he was not wealthy enough to become a member. "I was told by a friend that Opus Dei was only for people of culture and means," he said. "But then my wife started to go to talks by Opus Dei priests and I realised it was for ordinary people after all and I started to go to talks as well. I found it was a serious atmosphere, organised and inviting reflection on one's life," he said. "I believe God does not make mistakes and I came to feel he had chosen the founder, Monsignor Escrivá, to make this way for the sanctification of the lives of ordinary people. You see man is like the land, full of rocks and boulders, and it is hard to get anything to grow. But when you clean up the rocks, then you are able to plant. For me, Opus Dei has been good for cleaning up the rocks."

Bernardo said one of the things he had learned in Opus Dei was the danger of becoming a "Sunday Catholic": "I have learnt about this thing of unity of life, that you do not have to do strange things to be holy, but that your religious obligations do not stop when you leave the church after Sunday Mass." For instance, even though he went to Mass he used to look down on his workers because they were poor. "But Opus Dei has made me realise this attitude is wrong," he said. "It taught me to treat my workers better, with a spirit of service. Now I feel I understand them. We are like a family. We are at ease with each other." Bernardo mentioned a recent incident in which one of his prize bulls was accidentally killed. He said it had been a valuable animal and the meat had been worth a great deal. At first he had been determined to sell it, but then he decided his workers needed the meat more than he needed the money. There was nothing of self praise in the story. He said he was just grateful to God for helping him to see things that he had not seen before.

The Indians of Mexico have always occupied a special place in the Church. Many Catholics believe they were the reason for the Mother of God appearing as Our Lady of Guadalupe in the 16th Century soon after the Spanish first arrived. At the time Indians had been resentful and suspicious of the traders who came to their land and the efforts of missionaries to convert them to Christianity had failed. When the Virgin Mary appeared to a poor Indian named Juan Diego she left her image on the white cloth of his mantle. It was accompanied by a series of symbols which carried a clear message for the Indians. Within months millions converted. Among the unusual features of the image of Guadalupe is the longevity of the cloth it is impressed on: it has remained intact for centuries beyond its usual life span. The image is now venerated by Catholics all over the world and the Indians proudly point out: "God has done this for no other country."

The Church has been carrying out social works with the poor of Mexico for centuries. Religious orders in particular have done a great deal to further the cause of social justice amongst them. Members of Opus Dei consider the work they are doing as part of this tradition.

OPUS DEI

One project is being carried out high up in the mountains to the west of Mexico City beyond the city of Toluca at a hacienda called Toshi. This building was also given to Opus Dei members by an old Mexican family. Although it was in better condition than Montefalco, it also required renovation. Among the services it now offers to the local Indians are lessons on cooking and hygiene and a club for girls.

It was Sunday and Indian women were streaming in from all directions to buy food and clothing. The food was free, the clothing cheap, and there were doctors and nurses for anyone who needed attention. Some women came barefoot in their full skirts with babies strapped to their backs. Maria Gardunio, Juna Flores and Margarita Pacheco had walked for two hours. They came for milk and cheese for their children. Julian Carmona, an old man with a rough, lined face was almost blind. He was being led along on a donkey by his young granddaughter, Alicia. His wife, Leonor, said she came to Toshi regularly to learn to read and pray. Today she would also buy trousers for her husband.

Pascuala Martinez de Mejia, 69, a mother of 10, was a member of Opus Dei. She said she first came to Toshi to get milk for her baby back in 1960. At home she crushed corn, baked tortillas and took care of the cows and sheep and a donkey. At lunch time she took food to her husband in the field where they planted corn and wheat.

"Opus Dei has taught me to offer all of these things to God, to do them well and to pray," she said. "All of this was new for me. Before I went to Opus Dei I only knew how to make the sign of the cross.

"I learnt to do apostolate too. In these hills many people drink too much Pulque. They drink sometimes four bottles a day or more. They get drunk and they fight. They fight with their friends and their children. And then they don't make up. I try to teach them that they should not drink so much. And when they meet people they have had a fight with they should be polite with them and talk. They change a little bit, especially the ones who pray. They change and no-one knows why."

In one of Mexico City's poorest quarters there is an eye clinic for the poor which was founded by a kindly eye doctor, Dr Jose Prado, in the 1920s. The poor who go there are mostly suffering from eye infections caused by Mexico City's heavy pollution. With 400 patients a day the clinic has grown to be the largest of its kind in Latin America. Many members of Opus Dei now work there and it has an agreement with the Pan American University (a university in Mexico City founded by members of Opus Dei and their friends) for a much larger, jointly run clinic.

The Director, Dr Carlos Vidal, a member of Opus Dei, explained: "The reason we are working together with the university is because they share our goal: to give quality care to the poor. "The new project will mean the possibility of expansion. In the past we have only brought in enough funds to get by."

Dr Vidal said the idea for the university clinic came from the Prelate of Opus Dei, Monsignor del Portillo, who went to the clinic for treatment during a visit to Mexico. Dr Vidal said Monsignor del Portillo had encouraged the staff to do all they could to link the clinic with the university for the sake of the poor. "Opus Dei was begun on the prayers of the sick and the poor," he had said. "They are our treasure. We cannot loose them."

Dr Vidal added: "That is how the new clinic will be built, on the prayers of the poor. That is why we don't worry about the money, why we know it will come."

Coral Palmer had been working as an accountant at the clinic until the late 1970s when she became a social worker. She counsels the patients, particularly those who are blind. When people are about to lose their sight she teaches them to continue working. She explains to relatives how they can help. Coral has a special rapport with the blind because for several years she has been blind herself.

"I tell the patients not to stop fighting," she said, "to fight for their living, to fight to get a job or learn a trade so they are not a burden to their families. I tell them to always try to be happy and most of all I tell them they should build up their interior life and to offer everything to God."

One patient, 28-year-old Ricardo, had become depressed after he went blind. His father brought him to the clinic after he had tried to kill himself several times. Coral said she had advised him to go to a church at Santa Vera Cruz to speak to a priest. "At first he would not go," Coral said. "He said God did not exist and it was unfair that he was blind. But I told him that God was not unjust, that He was merciful, and that He didn't send this difficulty to him as a punishment. I told him God gave him his blindness as the best way for him to be saved and for his family to be saved as well. He is now at the society for the blind and he is learning braille and to play guitar. He is still going to Santa Vera Cruz and he is much happier.

Coral said if God gave her the choice of having sight or continuing to be blind she would continue as she is. "Being blind has given me another dimension, another meaning to my life. I am able to help more people this way. There are many people who have harder lives than me. There is one woman who comes here, a very poor woman who barely has enough to eat. Her name is Clarita. She doesn't even have enough money to pay for her visits to the doctor. She has glaucoma which is very painful. She is always in pain. She doesn't see with one eye and with the other she sees very little. But despite all of this Clarita says she feels God is giving her so much she has to go to Mass every day to thank Him. They tell me she wears a worn out skirt and tennis shoes and they say she always has a big smile. Every time she comes to see the doctor she brings me a gift, some candies or a rose. She is happy because she is close to God."

Although this chapter looks exclusively at Opus Dei's work with the poor, its work in Mexico is much wider. As in all countries that I visited it deals with people from all walks of life, But, as with the Church as a whole, it exercises a preferential option for the poor.

8

THE UNITED STATES
The urban poor

I F you walk from Chicago's Racine station on the L-train line, past the factories, the smoke stacks and the rusting cars to South Loomis Street you come to a pair of red brick buildings, Victorian terraces once owned by a member of Al Capone's gang. The only unusual thing about these two houses is that they are linked by a basketball court. There is nothing to indicate this is a place which has captured imaginations around the nation.

Inside, the main building is like a family home with its old polished wood staircase and lounge room with modern furniture, polished antiques, paintings and photos. The centre, Midtown, is a bold experiment in helping black and Hispanic kids get into college and succeed when they get there.

Even without Al Capone, Chicago's inner West Side with its racial neighborhoods—Hispanic Pilsen, Chinatown and the black ghettos—has always been one of the toughest areas in a tough town. One in 26 of the black youngsters you see walking the streets will die an early and violent death. At Midtown they have lost five students and one mother to gang warfare. The city's neighborhoods are sub-divided into gang strongholds marked out with symbols on buildings. Often the only safe way a youth can travel a few short blocks is by car or bus.

About 75 per cent of West Side youths have only one parent, half drop out of high school and the blacks and Hispanics have half the chance of graduating from college. During the summer vacation and after school Midtown has been trying to reverse this trend. It gives its students— Hispanics, Blacks and Asians—extra help with their studies, and career guidance. Sport also plays a big part at Midtown. A brochure on the centre's activities adds: "Once or twice a week, students have a chance to catch their breath, to talk with a counsellor on an individual basis and to reflect on the past and look to the future."

This last feature is a key part of the Midtown programme which seeks to strengthen students' characters as well as their intellects. The counsellors are chosen to act as role models to help motivate the youngsters. They are normally young men who have grown up in tough neighborhoods, but have managed to get ahead in life.

One of those who passed through Midtown and went on to a successful college career, Jimmy Palos, said: "There were guys more talented than me who got caught up in the gangs, playing war with chains, knives, guns. They were not bad guys. It was just the thing to do. They didn't have Midtown and they are still back there on the streets."

One student told a local newspaper: "If I hadn't gone to Midtown, I probably would have dropped out of school before now. I look at my old friends, and they're doing nothing now." He added that in the preceding two years two of his neighborhood friends had died in gang violence.

Another said: "I grew up on 18th Street. It's a Spanish ghetto now. If I hadn't gone to Midtown I might still be there. I don't think I would have set the goals for myself that I did."

"We try to challenge them," explained one of the workers at Midtown, Joe Major. "We try to open their eyes to their talents because many of them have very limited views of their possibilities in life. We give them extra training in academic subjects. We organise scholarships and financial resources. And we give them Christian development classes which are designed to be acceptable to everyone, Catholic and non-Catholic."

Around 64 per cent of Midtown students go to college. This compares with 30 per cent from Chicago neighborhoods as a whole. When they get there, the Midtown students have an almost 100 per cent success rate. Statistics like this have attracted attention, both locally and around the nation. Midtown now has the support of the Mayor of Chicago, has received funding from the federal government and visits from leading people in public life, including former president, Jimmy Carter, and his family. A local television station made a documentary on the centre called Pathways to Success.

Leo Gomez, a young psychology graduate, helps out at Midtown as a counsellor. Dressed in shorts and a t-shirt and wearing a cap with the peak at the back, his appearance does not fit the image of a professional psychologist. He is down to earth and animated in his speech, giving you the impression of someone who is passionate about his work: "I love counselling these kids because I was like them once," he said. "I don't like the idea of being an authority figure for them; I try more to be a friend. I kind of cringe at the thought of being a role model because I know I'm not perfect. But I try to make them understand they have a whole life ahead of them. The whole idea of Midtown is to make them see that eventually they can go to college and make something of themselves.

"A big part of helping them is just getting them to communicate. Sometimes the parents are a bit lost. They ask: 'What can I do?' I ask them if they ever talk to their son and I ask the kids: 'Do you talk to your mum about these things, about your friends and girls?' They think parents shouldn't know about these things, that they will over-react. So the trick is to get them to talk and the parents not to over react, just to sit and listen. That is all the kids really need, their parents to sit down and chat and ask 'How was your day?'. That is so important for a 6th grader.

"They are streetwise kids. You hear them talk about marijuana and coke and the gangs and all. You have to talk their language to get through. I tell them when they come here to use it to their advantage. The point of Midtown is to make them aware of the importance of their formation. I tell them now I am in the real world I know how important it is. All you can do is hope they will strive to do well. This is what it's all about for me. I think you really become a Christian when you start struggling. When you take those crosses up. I do it because if I don't I know from experience what I become. I become indifferent, I become arrogant and all the rest. And that is what I tell the kids: guys, you have got to struggle."

Luis Hymie and his wife, Petra, live in one of Chicago's poorest suburbs. A middle-aged couple, they have endured sickness, unemployment and poverty for many years, but it did not seem to have made them bitter. They explained how they had used their experiences to grow spiritually.

In the early 1970s Luis, a big man who had always worked with his hands, suffered a stroke. The doctors put the chances of survival at one in a million. There were three operations, all with negligible chances of success. Luis pulled through, but his kidneys failed. The family had been praying all this time and now they increased their efforts and the children prepared flowers to take to a local chapel of Our Lady of Guadalupe.

Mrs Hymie recalled that for a whole day at the hospital no doctor or nurse came near her because they believed her husband was ready to die. Then at three in the afternoon a doctor came and examined Luis. He called other medical staff to help him and he worked solidly until 8 o'clock when he emerged from the room and told Mrs Hymie that her husband was out of shock. When Mrs Hymie looked at the clock she realised it was the time when her children were at the chapel praying the Rosary. "I don't know why I did this," the doctor told her. "If he lives he will never be able to move or walk or talk. Nothing. He will be a vegetable. I don't know why I did this."

Luis came out of intensive care but the doctors still held no hope for his recovery. The hospital offered to pay for the nurses because they felt sorry for the family. "They were still convinced Luis was going to die," Mrs Hymie said.

Over a period of weeks Luis improved enough to be sent to a rehabilitation centre for tests. But the tests showed extensive and irreversible brain damage and the doctors confirmed the previous prognosis. They told Mrs Hymie to send Luis to a nursing home because he would never walk or talk; he would remain a vegetable.

"But we got him home," Mrs Hymie said. "It was then that a friend went to Venezuela to see Monsignor Escrivá who was visiting there. When he told Monsignor Escrivá about Luis he said that they had already talked to him about Luis and that a father who had been so generous with God, God would be very generous with him.

"We kept praying. The next appointment we had with the doctor he was amazed. He said he saw changes in him and it might be worthwhile to send Luis to therapy, something he had said he would never need. So Luis started getting therapy. It was like Luis was physically and mentally born again. He regained himself like a little child. After he started walking and everything the doctor told me: 'I don't know what you did and what happened, but this, it could not be possible.'

"Just to see the providence of God in these 10 years, how God has taken care of everything. So many things that have happened in our family. I never went to work and we were very, very poor. But the children were all able to stay in school. It was the divine providence and the help of Monsignor Escrivá—we would say the prayer of Monsignor Escrivá, all the children know it—we could never count up all the things that happened every day in our life. I think the children have learned so much from the situation of my husband and that makes us very happy."

Going back in time a little . . . before Luis fell ill the Hymies had nine children and they did not want any more. But then a priest reminded them it was good to be generous with God. "To tell you the truth, really, I wasn't pleased," Mrs Hymie said. "But we accepted the advice and left the matter to the will of God and it turned out to be God's will that we have two more children. And those two have been a blessing. Those two children . . . if it wasn't for them . . . Josemaría, the little one, he was one year old when my husband got sick, so they grew up together and it is so special the way—he respected his father—he took care of him . . ."

Luis: "One day I went up to the shop and got some cigarettes. You know I used to smoke before the stroke. Well I went to the porch here and I lit up the cigarette and I started smoking and little Joe come to me—he was about three or four years old—and he said: 'Dad, are you smoking?' I said: 'Yes.' 'You're not supposed to smoke,' he said, 'throw it away. You're not supposed to smoke. You know it will make you sick.'"

Mrs Hymie: "He knew how to take care of him. Because sometimes in his mind, Luis would think he could do everything. Little Joe respected him and at the same time he would take care of him and that is a very difficult combination. And he grew up with him like a friend. He played with my husband and he read to him and he tied his shoe laces and I think that he helped him so much to mature . . ."

Of his illness, Mr Hymie said: "In one way I am happy about it because at least, you know, I've got something to offer to God for my children, for my wife. It was hard you know, I could do nothing, I could not work, I could not do anything. Sometimes I feel bad because I can't even mow the lawn. But like I said, it made me happy in one way because I have something to offer. And because of what the children learnt of faith."

The Metro club near Midtown, runs programmes for girls similar to Midtown's. It was made possible partly by money from the US President's Inaugural Committee which chose 23 projects from thousands around the country for special support. Its classes include public speaking, Christian development, dance and career awareness. Students are mainly Hispanics, Blacks and Asians.

Programme coordinator, Margaret Black, said the club tried to get the girls off the street. Otherwise they would be pressured into gangs. Many thought only in terms of leaving school young and getting an assembly line job. About one in three fell pregnant before leaving school.

As with Midtown, the key to the Metro program is the personal counselling. For the girls their counsellor is often the only person "on the outside" they can talk to. "They know they are not alone," Margaret said. "They can get support for their goals in life." The result for most has been sharply improved grades at school. Some of the girls have gone from the bottom of the class to the top. For others the Metro has brought greater emotional stability.

The director of the Metro, Natalie Jakueyn, explained in the black culture of Chicago's West Side the whole concept of the family was almost non-existent. She said she and the others at the Metro were trying to help remedy that. Feedback from teachers, principals and parents had been good. "They say the girls are more outgoing and confident and positive about their work," she said. "Speaking to the girls one-to-one we try to lift their self esteem, their academic performance and their relationship with God."

THE UNITED STATES

I heard a similar story when I visited a centre similar to the Metro in New York, in one of the city's burroughs, the Bronx. For all of Manhattan's big-city coldness, going from 5th Avenue into the Bronx is like passing into an area ravaged by warfare. Everything was dirty, out of repair, decaying. Deserted apartment buildings with their rusting fire stairs and black interiors stood ghostly next to others which were still occupied; the only difference from the outside was the curtains in the windows.

The taxi driver, who had not been to the area for about 10 years, lost his way. We ended up in a dead-end street, surrounded by burnt-out tenements. Out of work men wandered aimlessly about the streets or sat on fences, staring. There were no whites to be seen. The engine failed twice in the heat and the driver started to get nervous. He was shaking so much he could not read his road map. Finally he decided to look for a police station to get directions. Turning to the passenger seat and eyeing my suit he asked irritably: "What the hell are you coming down here for anyway?"

Eventually we found our way to a small terrace house in East 174th St, formerly a family home and now the Rosedale club for girls. Since 1978 Rosedale has been helping young girls in the Bronx to do better at school and develop personally. In all, 500 girls have passed through. The people who run the centre see their main challenge in fighting the effects of broken homes, conflicts between children and their step parents, and drugs and violence.

"In many cases parents are not aware of their responsibilities," said Elizabeth Nonnemacker, a member of Opus Dei who helped establish Rosedale. "What we are aiming at is to strengthen the families. Many of our

127

programmes are geared towards 'home arts': helping families become aware of the dignity of the home."

In the late 1960s and early 70s the United States government tried to treat the problem of its ghettos by pouring money on it. As it turned out, money alone was not enough and some argue it actually aggravated the problem. It is now widely accepted the real stumbling block is the widespread lack of family life in these areas.

"Sometimes the family situation of the girls who come to Rosedale is terrible," Elizabeth said. "There is fighting and bickering at home and so we try to arrange things so the children go home happy and cheerful. And we encourage them to do things for their parents. For instance this week the girls are putting on a show for Mothers' Day. This kind of thing helps families to be more united. We also offer spiritual formation, classes in Catholic doctrine and days of recollection. There are courses for adults as well. Some have been baptised. Others have received their first holy communion."

New York is as brash, glossy and fast as any movie depicts it, a city where everyone seems to be chasing something and few look sideways. It brought to mind something a member of Opus Dei in Spain, Dr Jose Maria Barredo, had told me of the United States. He had migrated in 1946 and had stayed for 38 years. He said he found Americans were always in a hurry, and that the only place you could talk to them seemed to be on public transport. "I remember getting into the cab and starting up a conversation," he said. "We got on to spiritual things and after a while I realised we were not getting any closer to my destination. When I asked what the problem was the driver explained he had been driving

Main Building, University of Navarra, Pamplona.

The Center for Research and Communication, Manila.

Grandpont House, University of Oxford.

*Queen Elizabeth, The Queen Mother
at Netherhall House.*

Some youths at the Anchor Club, Dublin.

Southridge school, Manila.

Mother and son at Montefalco, Mexico.

Classes at the Toshi centre, north of Mexico City.

The author with Miguel Sinedo, Mexico.

Margarita Barranco, Mexico.

Midtown Center, Chicago.

Medical mission, Philippines.

The author with Cardinal Sin, Manila.

Monsignor del Portillo answers questions at a public gathering during his Australian visit in 1987.

around in circles. He said he didn't get much opportunity to talk, especially about serious things. He just wanted to talk."

One New York taxi driver, who picked me up outside Grand Central Station, told me he had been working in Manhattan for 20 years, ever since he migrated from South America. Now he said he was tired. He had been behind the wheel seven days a week for too long. "I'm 40," he said. "I want to go home to Colombia where people have time for other things. In Colombia I went to Mass every day. Here if I take the time off work to go on Sunday I am up to my neck with bills. Most New Yorkers only think about three things: work, money and number one. Work: we never stop! Everybody's always working. Money: that's all we want. And everybody is number one, and they think everyone else is no-one."

I spoke to several Opus Dei members in the US about coping with life in the country of "work, money and number one". One of them, Don Popp, was statistical Editor of a leading New York financial magazine. A short, stocky man, middle aged, with a crew cut and an energetic manner, he spoke of his attitude to work.

"I have this Jewish friend who is a very professional person," he began. "He really is a top guy. But he does not like work. He would rather sit home or go to the synagogue every day if he had the opportunity. He doesn't realise the value of work. So I was trying to get it across to him that work is good. Most people don't really see work as something of value in itself; and that really is a problem in our culture. Some people do everything they can to avoid work, even to the extent of working their tails off so they can enjoy retirement.

"We live in a culture today that wants everything. We have created needs for ourselves and people sacrifice many things for that 'good life'. They work two jobs, their wives work and all the rest. But it is always in order to do other things, to buy things. It seems no matter how much we make we never have enough. I've never met anybody who is satisfied with what they earn.

"The spirit of Opus Dei is really the thing that has helped me to get through all this: you know the idea that you should be detached from material things and working primarily to sanctify your work, to please Our Lord. That is my object; to please Our Lord in whatever I do. That does not mean I don't make errors. I am a statistician and I deal with thousands of numbers. I do make errors but I do the best I can. I've got to be honest: I enjoy my work enormously. I mean most of the work we do, after 25 years in this office, is the same as last year, the year before, or even as 25 years ago. But it does not bore me. Certainly work can be boring at times, but if you always keep in mind why you are working, that you are doing it for God and to serve other people, it becomes a joy.

"I try to improve the quality of my work, but my biggest desire is not to be the president of my company. My former boss who had the job I'm in now wanted to go on to bigger and better things. He is now making a lot more money and he wants to go higher and higher and higher. Well that's not for me. I'm more interested in staying where I am and being a good influence on those who work with me.

"The recognition that work can be God's work is so beautiful; to get this idea across to people, to me is exciting. That work can be the means of our sanctification whether it is physical work, from 9.00 to 5.00, or whether you are working around the house or playing sport. It is a revelation to many people, and I think it is catching on.''

Eric Streiff, a director of photography with a New York department store and a convert to Catholicism, and his wife Jolene, a former fashion designer, are raising a family in the suburbs, an unfashionable pastime with most of their counterparts. Eric said in New York it was usual for photographers to work 12 to 13 hours a day. Few were happily married. Like most New Yorkers Eric and Jolene lived a fast life, but, unlike many of their friends, they also had a home life. They decided having a family had priority over an apartment on 5th Avenue and a BMW. ''I think if we were both working full time and it was a matter of coming home to TV dinners and the rest I can see how my work might become my whole life,'' Eric said. ''I think this sort of thing is why many of the people I work with see work and professional success as where their fulfilment must lie, because they have no real fulfilment away from work. And that is why they are eventually so disappointed with it all. In my own case my family is a whole other world for me. I really look forward to going home at night.''

Jolene said starting a family in the high-pressure environment of New York was not easy: ''There were times when it would make you cry. But I found you just had to have faith in God and when you did, everything just fell into place. I think today people won't let God act. They want to do it all by themselves, to have complete control and they want everything immediately.''

Chris and Ann Woolf had a similar story to the Streiffs, a story of going against the fashion of the day and accepting

131

the children they were sent. Chris is Associate Professor of Constitutional Law at Marquette University and Anne, a Science graduate, mother and housewife. Anne said American culture was goal and achievement oriented, and becoming a full-time mother and homemaker meant foregoing the sort of public recognition that many of her friends received in the workplace. "You don't get any kind of recognition and you have to really be able to adjust interiorly," she said. "Opus Dei has helped me with that by teaching me to try to live each moment fully in the presence of God."

When the Woolfs started to have children Chris was at graduate school and they lived in a university town where it was "almost taboo" to have a child. "A lot of hostility was directed at me during that time," Anne recalled. "The zero population growth movement was very active and the prevailing attitude was that having children was the kind of thing that only people with very little education should do. So it was really hard and what I learned from Opus Dei helped me there too. I was advised to ask myself why the criticism upset me. And so I had to start to work through it and say: 'Well, what do I really believe and what would I profess no matter what everybody else does?' It was a great time for growing up. It helped to get out of the rat race of 'I've got to achieve what other people think is important; I've got to be on stage for other people and living for their approval'. Instead I learnt to get more my own sense of identity."

Chris: "Motherhood helps you do that too."

Anne: "Yes it does. And it is very helpful to have somebody to talk things over with. In spiritual direction one thing I find is you get much more realistic and a lot more forgiving of yourself and a little more sense of humour. For a mother it can be very hard to see some kind of meaning in the world when you are changing diaper after diaper and cleaning up dirty floor after dirty floor. But I find when you can think of Christianity as something through which every single detail of your life can be invested with meaning, it is all different. You know that while all these fragmented things may not make sense in themselves, they are all part of a pattern that gives tremendous meaning to your life. You are building an atmosphere where it is easier for people to develop their personality, where it is a little easier for them to grow spiritually. I suppose it is a matter of seeing it all as a managerial skill. You want to make the best environment for people to blossom. And then it becomes exciting to find ways to do it.''

Chris: ''I think this idea of giving a conscious supernatural orientation to your work is different to how most Americans view work. Before I met Opus Dei the idea of offering up work to God was a matter of having a kind of virtual intention of offering up work. Trying to make that a conscious idea throughout the day was very new. I suppose it gave me a better appreciation of the supernatural efficacy of work. I suppose I have the danger like many Americans of trying to be the best, in an unhealthy sense—wanting to stand out and be admired.

''I can be a very ambitious person for the wrong reasons. It is certainly good to try to do your best. One of the points in The Way for instance speaks of not having a 'barnyard vision'. But Opus Dei made me start to make distinctions between ambition for one's own ego and ambition for the glory of God and for the good of others. This is something I have been working on recently. I have recently published a book and it could conceivably be quoted by the Attorney General by the end of the year. Even before the book came out I was trying to pray the aspiration: 'All the glory for you God, not for me.' And that's certainly not something I would have done before.''

"Also, I find Opus Dei makes you want to take the faith to others in a natural sort of way. There is one fellow in my constitutional law class who was going to commit suicide because he was so down. And I started talking to him and just recently he came around and he said: ''I've got good news, I'm an alcoholic.'' And it was good news because he could admit it. I'm trying to give him support and encouragement and if it helps him grow in a religious sense, then that's good too. There are all sorts of ways of doing apostolate—I mean helping people see things as they are . . .''

Finally, there was Jack Burns, a middle-aged telephone linesman who lives in a working class neighborhood on Chicago's West Side. He was a solidly built, outdoors type with a sense of humour. When he became a member of Opus Dei his wife Dorothy was impressed enough by the effect on her husband to look into Opus Dei and eventually joined herself.

Jack: "For me Opus Dei is just trying to sanctify my life and my family and trying to encourage others to do the same. On the job I try to set an example for the others and to get to know each one personally. That's my apostolate—to get to know people. They often need advice, the men I work with, and so you tell them how you think. I mean you don't want to be preaching on the job, but if you do it in a natural way . . .''

Dorothy: "The thing that impressed me when Jack got

involved with Opus Dei was he was so much more help around the house. We had six children and it seemed all of a sudden it dawned on him that mum needed help and it made for really pleasant home life.

"He was playing baseball three nights a week and so he gave that up. He used to come home and give the children a bath. It might sound little but it was really a big thing. So that made me think. It really impressed me."

Dorothy: "When you have a family you can be kind of overwhelmed by it unless you have a good interior life. That gives you the serenity and you are able to cope with things more. I see a lot of people and they worry and they fret and they stew about a lot of things. My experience is if you pray about things they are resolved in a better way. Not everything turns out the way you want, but it really does help to pray. People think they have to be in control of every little thing. I'm afraid I just leave it to God to do the worrying and do what I can.

"There is so much in America that can lead you away from God and from the faith, so many material things and so many ideas that are trying to lead you away from God. I was reading an article once in a women's magazine by a Catholic woman with a PhD. She was carrying on about why she was only going to have two children. Jack looked at it and he said: 'You know, she doesn't mention God here at all.' And I looked again and he was right. It was all: 'What I want, what I want.' "

Jack: "It's the subtleness you see. People write their articles and it all sounds great. But then when you reflect on things you realise they are always leaving God out or bending things to suit themselves. Take me. I like to fish and that sounds harmless too, but if I get hung up on fishing and it's diverting me away from my spiritual life and my family . . .

"We are all going fishing in June, the boys and the neighbours. It's good, something you can enjoy. And at the same time it is a chance to talk to the others about how their lives are going and try to help them out if you can. You can also do a lot of drinking on a fishing trip, so that is something I'll have to watch . . ."

9

THE PHILIPPINES
The poor of the third world

MANILA'S poor live in tiny shacks of scrap wood and rusting tin on mud. Even those not in squatters' settlements are in tiny houses of one or two rooms. One home was no more than a few weathered boards between the branches of a tree.

Like their counterparts in other countries Manila's poor left the land where they were often exploited and headed to the city looking for a better life only to be disappointed. In the poorest areas morality is low, sometimes non-existent. It is not unusual for a youth to have seen several murders before he has reached maturity.

The Philippines has been a troubled country since the 19th Century when it began to strive for independence. Most recently the country has suffered from a stifling dictatorship.

It was against this background that the People's Power revolution came about in 1986. After the dust of the uprising settled the effects of the years of dictatorship remained. One figure tells the story: 70 per cent of Filipinos live below the poverty line.

At my lodgings in Manila, a small apartment building in San Juan, one of the oldest areas of the city, there was an armed guard in blue stationed at the entrance. His presence was a reminder of the desperate poverty all around.

Confronted with this suffering many Christians assume the only choice is between doing what Mother Teresa of Calcutta does—going out into the streets and ministering directly to the poor themselves—or giving to those who do. But even Mother Teresa recognises charity is only a temporary cure. Another response to the problem actively promoted by the Church is the way of social justice based on Christian social principles. It is a way that seeks to avoid the extremes of exaggerated profit capitalism on one hand and totalitarian systems on the other.

It was this alternative, the challenge proposed by the Church's social teaching, which a small band of Filipino university students had taken up long before the 1986 revolution. When they came together in the mid 1960s, they were aware that although the Philippines was a predominantly Catholic country, it had paid little heed to the Church's social teachings. They were young men, without social, political or economic influence; all they had was their education and their youth. Two members of that initial group were Dr Bernardo Villegas and Dr Jesus Estanislao, both economics graduates from Harvard.

"We wanted to create a social service which would be both professional and secular and which would answer the most pressing social needs," Jess said. "It had to be educational, apostolic and open to everyone because we wanted to reach out to as many people as possible."

The group set out to show that corporations could be socially responsibile. But one of the first hurdles was the fact that the government was going one way and business was heading in another. While the government spoke of social and economic programs, it had very little communication with private enterprise. On the other hand business was only interested in making profits, not in social and economic development.

"We wanted to have a center which would research these things and communicate to both government and private enterprise," Jess said.

The result was the Center for Research and Communication, which opened in 1967 at rented premises at 1607 Jorge Bocobo, Malate—a far cry from the centre's latest home, a modern building at Pearl Drive in Manila's Ortigas Commercial Complex, with its modern seminar rooms, lecture halls and offices. Soon after its birth, the CRC gained a reputation as a dependable business training center offering courses in economics and as a think tank giving economic forecasts. (The center's economic forecasts came to be resented by the government which did not appreciate an independent body highlighting the ailing country's poor economic performance). The CRC trained businessmen to run their businesses on sound economic principles. And then it urged them to try to identify areas where they could help combat poverty—to respond to the Church's "preferential option for the poor". For instance, it asked each company to find out the real incomes of its own workers, the money they had available to give their families food and shelter; if the employers did not have the figures the CRC supplied them.

Bernie explained: "What we have always said to the different firms is: 'This is what your employees get and this is what they need to live as human beings'. Then we have gone one step further. Take rural development for example. If a client is operating a sugar mill we tell him he must make sure he is helping to develop the community, by putting up schools, hospitals, and so on. There is a common belief around that capitalism is without any conscience. That is what we have been seeking to disprove. We are trying to make business aware of everything that the Church has said about wages, about labour unions, work, cooperatives and all the social problems that a third world country like the Philippines has. We have found that those businesses we have been able to reach are ready to listen once they understand the problems and that they can do something about them."

Businesses which came to the CRC for economic advice soon began to respond. Some began to expand into rural areas to contribute to rural development; others established foundations for the training of technical workers or farmers; some produced high quality products which helped the poor economise. Meanwhile the CRC pressed for land reform, encouraging large landholders to divide up their lands into parcels for small farmers.

"The message we have always tried to put across," said Jess, "is that in business before we start looking into the distance, into the future, we must remember the poor are with us, that they are our drivers, our janitors, our clerks, our farmers. We have insisted that corporate executives must take care of these people first, give them an opportunity for further education, treat them very well, provide for their necessities in terms of their cultural, spiritual, professional, educational development; to take care of their material advancement too, within the resources of the company. Those who have looked into it closely have found this approach works both ways. When corporations take good care of people a close affinity is established between the corporation and its employees. The corporate operations become viewed as a joint venture between the lower level people, the owners and top management. As a result, productivity increases."

The social doctrine of the Catholic Church has always rejected the notion that the solution to economic ills lies in ideologies such as socialism, capitalism or liberation theology. What the CRC was doing was based on three basic pillars. First, the principle of subsidiarity, which says what can be done competently and efficiently by individuals or by small groups should not be absorbed by larger bodies, least of all by the State. (This is the approach which has become popularly known as the "small is beautiful" approach. It requires that all workers should be part owners in the great work bench of production.) Second, the principle of solidarity, which says that individuals and private groups and associations should always work in unity and cooperation. The third principle is that each individual and group in the community should try to work for the common good. This does not mean seeking the greatest good for the greatest number, but rather the total good of each and every member of society.

"This is where CRC's distinctive competence comes in," Bernie said. "There are other institutions like CRC doing economic business research but I think we stand out for the emphasis on the principles of subsidiarity, solidarity and the common good. We are making it very clear to businessmen that there is no invisible hand, nothwithstanding what Adam Smith said, that automatically promotes the common good if you encourage individuals to be selfish. That is the biggest lie in economic history. Each individual must consciously and actively contribute to the common good through each decision they make.''

All of this might seem attractive idealism but not really practical in a world where businesses strive to extract as much profit from their workers as possible to survive. In fact the opposite is true. Companies which exploit workers and make big profits in the short term are sowing the seeds of their own demise. The CRC has been able to convince enough hard-headed businessmen of this fact of life to attract widespread support. A tour of the building on a busy day reveals packed lectures, seminars and conferences. Every six months briefings are given at the Manila hotel to hundreds of businessmen.

Even though the people at the CRC are united in promoting basic principles, they sometimes have different views about how these can be put into practice. The centre stresses that the economic opinions of its staff are their own responsibility. For example, though Jess and Bernie have worked together for many years they have different views on how to tackle the Philippines' economic problems in several areas. Bernie believes ''agribusiness'' is the key to the future. Jess emphasises rehabilitating industry and preparing for a new phase of industrialisation. They also have different opinions about tariff protection. Each respects the others opinion, but they have agreed to disagree.

Bernie summed up: ''Here we have a great pluralism of

opinion, the idea that it is not right to issue dogmas in economics. As the founder of Opus Dei said, in Opus Dei we have a common denominator which is everything the Church teaches as doctrine. But our numerator is completely varied: we have all sorts of views on how to tackle particular problems. That is true of Opus Dei and it is true of the CRC.

"The same goes for those we advise. No-one has the authority to dicatate how a person with surplus wealth may contribute to the common good, whether by creating employment opportunities, by earning much needed foreign exchange for the country, by producing food products for the masses, or whatever. Personal freedom and responsibility should be the main propeller of private initiatives to promote the common good."

Opus Dei's part in what happens at the CRC is the same as in any other corporate work. It guarantees the doctrine and the spiritual guidance that is given, and all that is taught conforms with the Catholic faith. Nothing more. It takes no reponsibility for things like forecasting exchange rates or opinions on whether land reform should be introduced in the island of Negros.

The resident chaplain at the CRC, Fr Hector Raynal, spoke about the advice he gave businessmen who came to him to talk about their spiritual lives.

"In this country people take their religion for granted," he said. "The people are good but they don't go deeply into the knowledge of the teachings of Jesus Christ. We have to go through the basic things with them first: the sacraments, the need for the state of grace, very basic things. Then there is a need for an awareness of human virtues: hard work, determination, constancy, perseverence, sincerity—all of these things."

"I try to make people who come here aware that if they want to build a society along Christian lines they have to get to know what the Church has taught. If you build a society, even if you are very successful economically, and it is not based on correct moral principles, it is bound to fail. Either you build with too much materialism, too much concern for material goods, or you build on a structure which does not allow for the rights of the individual. Either way, you are building on sand. You will end up with nothing.

"If someone comes to me here to ask whether it is moral to enter a particular business deal I will try to help. In fact I give a course on Christian morals for businessmen which gives clear guidelines based on the laws of God. Say someone comes along and says: 'We are in this situation: we have to cope with competition which does not pay taxes, which issues cheques which bounce, which pays lower than the wages established by law and which bribes officials. We have to compete with them. What do we do? Can we do the same things they are doing?' You have to advise them: 'Definitely not!' So then do they bow out? No. Not necessarily. You have to study the situation. This is where the faith comes in. Granted you can't do the same things that the unscrupulous do. You cannot avail yourself of illicit means, because the end does not justify the means. But bowing out means just losing out the world, leaving it in the hands of those who are hurting it. So you must see if you can make use of other means which are licit and are powerful and that the competition does not have. The spirit of Christ tells us we must place Christ on the top of human activity, that we must consecrate the world back to God. How are we going to do that if every time we have difficulties we bow out because we are afraid of the situation. We must make use of the licit means which happen to be very powerful. I mean prayer coupled with the possibility that maybe you will have to work harder.

"I tell them they have to turn their company into a more efficient one, yes, but not to think that because they are Catholics and they cannot make use of illicit means, that they are always going to end up at the tail end of every single transaction. That idea, that in order to be a good Catholic you have to be a beggar, is old fashioned, and wrong. That was one thing Monsignor Escrivá wanted to change in the minds of individuals—that it is wrong to be a person who is putting up a fight. On the contrary you have to be better than the best and you have to be successful like your peers. And this is important too in order for you to be able to spread the Gospel.

"So that is more or less the advice I would give: to fight. But if somebody comes to me and asks me if they should join a particular political party then that is not my area, that is not my responsibility—as long as you don't overstep the limits set up by the Church, as long as you don't, for example, join the Communist Party, you are free to do whatever you like to help solve the problems of your country. That is up to you. You are absolutely free."

Today the CRC has 80 workers, including several senior economists 12 junior economists and about 20 research staff. In recent years it has started to evolve into a university specialising in economics, business, journalism, education and the humanities. Already it has started preparing an academic staff, many of whom are studying at overseas universities.

It might seem that of all the corporate activities of Opus Dei looked at so far, the CRC would be a prime target for the charge of seeking worldly influence. The staff at the centre said they were happy to be judged on their record, that in the long term people would not make up their minds on the basis of rumours, but on facts.

This is also the view of the Archbishop of Manila, Cardinal Jaime Sin. Not long before we spoke at his Manila residence Cardinal Sin had written an article in a local newspaper defending Opus Dei, the work of its members in his own diocese and particularly the CRC.

It was important, Cardinal Sin said, to appreciate that the CRC was not a political group, but a professional one. "When you are studying financial problems and planning for the future you are not working for any political party," he said. "You are working for the welfare of the country. That is very clear. The CRC gives a great help to the government through their analysis and evaluation of financial problems. They have shown they have foresight and planning, that they are experts who work in a very professional way. So this has meant the government takes notice of what they do and in this way they are helping to improve and develop the country."

Cardinal Sin pointed out when the previous dictatorship ended and a new government took over in the Philippines the CRC remained as it was before, doing the same work and advising the same people, including the new government: "This is good policy," he said, "because the moment the Church, or any organisation for that matter, marries the system, that organisation will become a widow in the next generation. That is clear." This approach of course is followed by the Church, not only because it protects the Church from being compromised in a political sense, but because it protects the freedom of lay members of the Church.

THE PHILIPPINES

Two projects inspired by the CRC are Dual Tech, a worker training centre, and the Meralco Foundation industrial technicians programme. Both seek to provide opportunities for the poorest workers.

Dual Tech, in the Makati business district of Metro Manila, is a joint venture between the Southeast Asian Science Foundation, a non-profit organisation, and the West German Hanns Seidel Foundation. It was launched by a group of businessmen because some firms were not giving their skilled workers proper training. Dual Tech has two basic aims: first, to adapt a German dual teaching system combining on-the-job training with classroom teaching; and second, to encourage good attitudes and values, both on the job and in personal life.

Trainee mechanics and industrial electricians are chosen from disadvantaged areas all over the country. For the first six months of their studies they are given free meals and medicine. For some this is the first time they have eaten regularly in their lives. They have come from areas where they received little moral training or religious instruction. One of the instructors at Dual Tech, Florentino Fernando, said it was an environment where killing was not something of shame, but something to be boasted about. "What saves most of those who come to us is their faith," he said. "In spite of everything they want to do better. They know the basics. They know if they rape or kill someone it is wrong. But they don't know much more. And they are aware that they need to learn if their lives are going to improve."

In the work values course the trainees are taught basic human virtues, partly through group discussions, group dynamics games and talks. Each trainee has a personal counselor who tries to help lift his horizons little by little and this is often where the most valuable work is done.

Florentino spoke of some of his own experiences as a counselor. He said he had recently given a talk on the importance of family life and one of his students came to him afterwards with a problem: "I think my wife knows I am seeing another woman," he said. Florentino said he had only been talking about small things, about the importance of taking care of the children and giving more time to your wife, but this fellow's conscience had been pricked. When Florentino asked him if he was willing to change he said he was because he realised his family was important. "So I asked him if he was willing to stop seeing the other woman," Florentino said. "He wanted to, but he thought it would be difficult. He showed me a gold necklace the other woman had given him. He had told his wife he was paying it off at 200 pesos a month, which also helped him to give the other woman money regularly. I advised him the only way to do it was to cut the relationship off totally and completely. He did not look happy but he seemed to accept the advice. He came back to see me a month later and he was smiling. He looked different. He had had a hair cut and he had cleaned himself up. He said: 'Good news. I gave back the necklace.' He had stopped seeing the woman. 'You know,' he said, 'its surprising, but I feel very light now. I appreciate my children and wife more.' This man had made mistakes but you could see he was basically good. He had a quality. It was obvious it had taken a lot to give up that woman."

The Meralco project in Metro Manilla has many similar features to Dual Tech. It raises the professional qualifications of poor workers and helps them improve their personal life. It offers a 3-year post secondary course in electronics or instrumentation technology for about 120 young men and women. The qualifications are a good academic record and poverty. Meralco provides free tuition, books, materials, uniforms, a travelling allowance and a wage. One trainee, Bernardino Equitay, 24, grew up as a farm boy on the island of Negros, one of the most impoverished areas in the Philippines. His father grew rice and corn, supporting six children on 1,000 pesos ($A90) a month. When he left the farm he did a business training course but found out afterwards that it did not qualify him for a job. "One of the things I like about Meralco," he said, "is that when the training is over I am assured of getting a job."

Another project with the poor of Manila is the Punlaan school and technical institute at San Juan which provides professional courses for women who work in household administration in private homes, hotels, restaurants and hospitals.

Since it began with 115 students in 1975 Punlaan has enrolled more than 2500 students and has become a consultant on curriculum planning to the Ministry of Education, Culture and Sports. The school, housed in a former hospital building in M. Paterno St, is spotlessly clean and tastefully furnished.

The Directress, Miss Amy Bonotan, explained the aim of the school was to try to make students aware of the beauty of household work. "We show them there can be dignity in their work and help them understand they don't need to be ashamed of it," she said.

Students at Punlaan pay no more than 60 pesos ($A5) a month which does not cover the cost of their education. A foundation raises the rest. There is a basic one-year course or a more advanced two-year college-level course which leads to a diploma and the possibility of a career in restaurant or hotel catering. Besides the usual subjects there are some that are unusual for this kind of institution, subjects like character development, history, ethics, government, writing and psychology.

"The girls are from poor, really poor families, living below the poverty line," Amy said. "We help them realise their work is not something low, that it is a service which is high if it is done well and we help them to develop as human persons. We teach them they can grow through their work."

One problem for household workers in the Philippines has been exploitation and abuse by employers. The staff at Punlaan are working with the government to create laws to protect them. "The girls must have justice and respect from their employers," Amy said. "They have a right to privacy, to free speech, to an education and good working conditions.

"We hold seminars for employers and we try to make them more sensitive to the way they deal with their workers. You see the girls are not well educated and they tend to think more with their feelings. They are easily offended. This is where the regular meetings with their counsellors here at the school can be a great help. The girls learn to talk about their feelings and to get over some of their hurts.

"This does not mean the flow is all one way. They teach us lessons as well. Sometimes I am amazed by their wisdom. It is really something. You can't get it from books. They have had difficult lives and have come through hard times. The strength they show in confronting those situations is inspiring. They really fight poverty and have a deep faith.

"There is one girl who has undergone many difficulties. Her parents did not care for her and she had transferred from one employer to another. When she came here she felt it was her only chance of a future. But she says she believes all of the things she has been through have helped to make her stronger. She is not bitter at all. Another girl had an employer who was not upright. When she came here she was afraid and down hearted. But she explained her problem to the tutor who was able to rectify the situation."

Most of my time in Manila was spent looking into what was being done to help Filipinos who are materially poor. But there was also the other side of Opus Dei's mission, the work with the spiritually poor.

Benjamin Defensor is a former journalist with Time Magazine and editor of a string of newspapers in the Philippines including Business Day. He was forced to live in Hong Kong during the years when the Philippines was under martial law. There he became an editor with Asia Television Limited. It was in Hong Kong that he met Opus Dei. He described himself up to that point as a "rough fellow"—a heavy drinker, with little interest in the spiritual life.

"Even after I got married I used to come home at 2 o'clock in the morning," he said. "I used to tell my friends: 'I might be married, but I am not changing my lifestyle'." So it went on for many years. But after he met Opus Dei he stopped drinking. He said he also overcame a lifelong habit of worrying, particularly about money: "I was told just to pray and trust in God," he said. "I haven't worried about money for years and everything has always seemed to work out fine."

Teofilo San Luis Jnr. a specialist in nuclear medicine at the hospital at the University of St Thomas told me that before he met Opus Dei, every morning as he drove through the hospital gates he would start to feel ill just thinking about the day ahead. "I looked on it as the daily grind, something that came and went, day in and day out," he said. "Life had little meaning." There was the opportunity of working for the poor in the hospital's charity section, but that did not attract him. It seemed futile, a waste of time. He said since he came into contact with Opus Dei he found his outlook had changed. "I realised how important it was to devote yourself to helping people. So I decided to try working in the charity section one day a week. After that I no longer saw patients as sources of income. I started to share people's problems. I try to spend more time with patients, giving them advice help, even encouraging them to pray. Now I don't get that feeling that I used to get on my way to the hospital in the morning."

Dr Marina Bringas, a mother of five, working at the Quezon City General Hospital, told a similar story of recovering from spiritual dryness: "Before, I used to try not to get involved with patients," she said. "I was only interested in the technical things. These days it is different. Some mothers come to the charity ward and sleep on the floor to be with their sick children and I try to spend time with them. Some I encourage to pray. Or if a patient is in pain I suggest offering it up to Our Lord. They are only small things, but they have meant a big change for me. It is all part of doing your work as well as possible, of consciously offering it to God."

Sergio Sanchez, a corporate pilot flying Hawker 125 jets for the Filipino firm, Anscor, said Opus Dei taught him to stop thinking about himself. Previously, he said, he would always make certain he got the best flights. He had learnt instead to volunteer for the worst flight with the most obnoxious passengers. "I was self-centred, you know." I have been taught to try to think of others more, without letting them know. Sometimes that meant allowing the other pilot to take a longer flight because he needed the extra money. Sometimes it meant helping someone think more of God. "You know when you are flying there is a very strong feeling of being close to God," Sergio said. "Sometimes you are so high you can see the curvature of the earth and it is so beautiful. It also makes you feel vulnerable—all pilots are very aware that their life could end very quickly. They talk about it a lot. And there is the awareness that something is holding you in existence, the same thing that powers the plane and the instruments, and it is all so delicately poised. This is a very good environment for doing apostolate, for speaking with another person about deeper things. Many of my colleagues have been to talks and meditations at centers of Opus Dei and some are now members."

Finally Monina Mercado, a former journalist, now Editor-in-Chief of Gabriel Books and a mother of three, described herself as a lady of the early 60s. "I loved those times: the music and the social life, the exhibits, cocktail parties and concerts," she said. "But, although it was not an immoral lifestyle, it was frivolous and I used to feel futility. There is an expression 'ashes in the mouth' and that is what I felt. Even though I loved it all, the laughter and the feeling I was amongst the 'important people' who were deciding the future of the world, I was deeply unhappy.

"It is not that there is anything wrong with parties and cultural things of course. But it is wrong for your whole life to be centred on seeking after pleasure. Since I started practising the faith seriously I find I don't need the frivolous things I used to think I needed. And I realise how much more important my role as a mother is. There are still many difficulties in life of course, but I no longer have those ashes in the mouth. Since I started practising the faith seriously I find I don't need the frivolous things I used to think I needed. And I realise how much more important my role as a mother is. There are still many difficulties in life of course, but I no longer have those ashes in the mouth.''

10

AUSTRALIA
The witness of others

ON Wednesday, June 5, 1974, a mob of university students led by a man dressed as the devil marched in funeral procession on Warrane College, at the University of NSW in Sydney. Four hooded pall bearers laboured under a black coffin inscribed: Opus Dei RIP. Another group carrying crosses and wearing masks and hoods began a mock exorcism.

The incident is often referred to in articles about Opus Dei in Australia. One journalist wrote that Opus Dei was subsequently banned from the campus. Another blandly reported that an investigation took place without giving any account of the circumstances which led to it or the result.

So what actually happened?

Tension over Warrane had been building on campus for

155

some time. This was despite the fact that college residents did not back the opposition to college rules. A majority of them signed a letter to the Vice-chancellor of NSW University, Sir Rupert Myers, "deploring" attacks on Warrane and disputing criticism of its management. Past residents, parents and others came to Warrane's defence.

Nevertheless, the demonstration went ahead. After burning an effigy of the Master of the college, Dr Joe Martins, the demonstrators called on Dr Martins to come out and answer to them. When their demands were not met they changed tactics and marched on the university's Chancellory building. There they occupied a meeting room and confronted the acting Vice-Chancellor, Professor V.C. Vowels. A long debate followed with the demonstrators demanding Opus Dei's influence at Warrane be brought to an end.

At the centre of the demonstrators' discontent was one of the college's rules, the one which forbade residents taking women to their bedrooms. This was out of line with the new moral "enlightenment" reflected in the columns of the local campus student newspaper, Tharunka. The paper carried pornographic and blasphemous material and preached energetically the new gospel of sexual liberation.

At that time student protests were not unusual. To be sure, there had been some important issues in the past, such as Australia's involvement in the Vietnam war. But now issues to fuel the machinery of radical student politics were fewer. Student newspapers of the time show the fashionable causes were all off campus, most of them centred overseas. As far as the local campus went, it was a case of radicalism looking for somewhere to happen. In this atmosphere Warrane was made an issue. The cry of "puritanism and authoritarianism" went up and the radicals were on the march again.

As the confrontation developed in the university's chancellery between demonstrators and the acting Vice-Chancellor, its true nature became more clear. It was clearly a test of strength between radical students and the university's administration. As Tharunka proudly boasted later, the demonstration "showed that students can be a force within this university." The Tharunka report spelt out the situation further: "As long as the university is controlled by conservative forces of administrators, business interests and senior staff, students will never have real power with the university." In the event, the will of the students prevailed. Professor Vowels promised an investigation.

The next day it was all in the Sydney press and in the weeks that followed a debate sprang up in newspaper letters columns both on and off campus. One man wrote: "I know nothing about Warrane College and Opus Dei but what I have read in your paper (Tharunka). On that evidence alone, your anti-Opus Dei campaign has rather appalling implications. Stripped of their rhetoric, the objections in Tharunka to Warrane College policy boil down to (a) they are Catholic; (b) they don't let students visit with maids or girls in rooms; (c) they expel students for breaking rules or promoting pornographic movies; (d) they hang crucifixes on walls." The writer, Lawrence J. Dickson, went on to observe: "The rhetoric and cartoons (used in Tharunka's article on the college) make rather obvious the real reason behind this campaign. The far left-wingers and 'sexual freedom' supporters cannot tolerate a bit of the campus which dares to reject their standards. They are even willing to resort to mob action to drive such a dissenting group off campus. This is academic freedom?"

When the Vice-chancellor, Sir Rupert Myers, returned from

an overseas trip he found he had been left with no alternative but to support an inquiry. After meeting with the university's governing Council he appointed a committee. Even the student leader at the time had to admit, in print, that the panel was as "balanced as a butcher's scales".

The inquiry began on July 8, 1974. Members included senior academics, the Vice-chancellor himself and NSW Supreme Court judge, Mr Justice Samuels. The committee did not extend any special priveleges to the college. In fact it said in its report that it had adopted the approach that it was more important to talk to the critics rather than to college supporters.

The final report found discontent over Warrane was inspired by those whose attitudes and beliefs were fundamentally opposed to the Christian approach of Opus Dei. It condemned the idea that Warrane's management was narrow and rigid as a "value judgment incapable of rational demonstration". It said the college had been founded "to promote education and the development of character in accordance with the principles and ideals of Christianity" and pointed out the university, which invited Opus Dei to establish the college, could not contend that its aims were "other than proper and deserving of support."

In retrospect, perhaps the most interesting aspect of the whole affair was the committee's investigation of the claim by militant students that Opus Dei's aim and philosophy were, as the committee described it, of a "more ambitious and secular kind", a similar claim to the one investigated by the Italian Government in 1986. The inquiry left no room for doubt on its attitude to this allegation:

"There is no evidence before us capable of supporting the suggestion that Opus Dei has employed its position on the campus as a means of bringing its corporate influence to bear upon any institution of the university. Equally, there is no evidence which would justify the conclusion that Opus Dei, either on or off the campus, is an organisation which designs by secrecy and stealth to overthrow existing institutions, or to infiltrate, for its own purposes, positions of power and responsibility.''

The inquiry added that the material before it did no more than establish that Opus Dei was "the lay apostolate which it purports to be."

The uproar was over. There were no more protests.

Warrane College, which is run by a non-profit company, Education Development Association (E.D.A.), has an eight-member council which has included people who are not members of Opus Dei and non-Catholics. According to the Regional-Vicar of Opus Dei in Australia and Warrane's first chaplain, Fr John Masso, the motivating idea behind Warrane is expressed in a wall hanging in the college's library—the great commandment: "That you love one another." Warrane staff encourage students to see their future profession as a service to others and to help create a family atmosphere at the college. The college has academic tutors, but older students also help younger ones with their studies. There are get togethers at night in the college's common rooms, social functions throughout the year and residents are encouraged to take part in sport. Staff say they try to involve parents in the life of the college as much as possible; every year a parents weekend is held to keep parents in touch with the life of the college.

Despite the early problems on campus Warrane has been well received by the Australian public. Visiting speakers who address students once every week have included top people from government, industry, the press, sport and the arts. Among them have been the man destined to become Federal Treasurer in the Hawke Labor government, Mr Paul Keating, Attorney General in the same government, Mr Lionel Bowen, the designer of the wing keel on Australia II, the yacht which won the Americas cup, Ben Lexen, cartoonist Larry Pickering and many others. As well as its work with university students, Warrane also organises sporting camps for school students and work experience and university orientation camps for country students.

Following are three reactions to Warrane by people who are not members of Opus Dei.

Journalist with the Sydney Morning Herald, Alan Gill, in a three-part series on Opus Dei in Australia wrote: "I have visited Warrane four times and was impressed by the excellent living and working conditions, the obvious contentment of the majority of students, the highly developed system of tutorials and the general tone of the environment."

Noel Ling, 51, an elder of the Presbyterian Church and chief executive of China Development Council, a company developing free enterprise projects in China, is a former bursar of Warrane College. He came to the college in 1978. "The first moment I met them (members of Opus Dei) and saw what they were doing I thought our goal was the same," he said. "Without going into the theology of it, the general principle is the same and probably is the same for all Christians."

Noel became Warrane's desk attendant because he wanted

160

a job which would give him more free time to spend with his young son. Later he was made Bursar. Over the years he says he has made many friends among members of Opus Dei, travelling overseas to attend the ordination of two of them: Father Paul Grant and Father Tony Khoudair. He said he did not work at the college for the financial reward— 'you don't come to Warrane to get rich" - but because he liked the work it was doing and the principles it stood for.

"There are certain points of doctrine involved in Opus Dei that are different from my church, but we don't talk about those," he said. "If you were to find a hundred things to talk about I would say about 90 would be the same. You just don't talk about the other things because it is not necessary. It all boils down to the fact that Opus Dei has ideals and a way of doing things I admire."

Dr Ben Haneman, 63, is a consultant physician, Jewish and a member of his local synagogue. He is also a member of E.D.A. and President of the Warrane Association. At the height of the controversy over college rules he wrote to the Sydney Morning Herald defending the college in the following terms: "At the outset I want to make it clear that I am a Jew and not a Catholic, that I am a socialist, and that I have tremendous sympathy and affection for students. I became a member of the college board because I have tremendous admiration for the work this college is doing. It has been my passionate belief that not only is there room for Warrane at the University of NSW, but also that the university has need of Warrane. I believe that this college can make a significant contribution to the life and work of the university.

"I believe that Warrane's opponents have singled it out

because it takes a spiritual rather than a materialistic position. Not everyone will accept that explanation. The explanation that will be offered in its place will be student unrest because women are not allowed in the residents' bedrooms.

"When I was young—and I've now turned 50—the rule Warrane has now regarding women visitors was accepted as utterly reasonable. I know very well that this is no longer acceptable to many students. But if a student has a need to live in a mixed college, he can go to any of the other six colleges on campus, which are all mixed and live there."

When we spoke, Dr Haneman recalled the battles for Warrane in the early 70s: "There was certainly some strange psychology driving those people (the demonstrators)," he said. "Some of them were lapsed Catholics, but there was also at that time still anti-Catholic feeling amongst some Protestants in this country. My wife is a Protestant, but I always thought the Opus Dei people were doing a good job. And also from a broad point of view, I believed Australia needed Opus Dei's contribution to its thinking. In a very materialistic world it was refreshing to find people who thought the way they did. Without going into the theology of it, I found them sincere and a great example. And I thought Warrane was a beautiful college. It has a very nice feel to it. I like walking into the place."

Opus Dei began in Australia when Fr Jim Albrecht and Fr Chris Schmidt, arrived from the United States in 1963. They were followed by five lay people from the States and from Spain. A professor of Engineering at NSW University, Dr Ron Woodhead, had met up with Opus Dei while visiting Boston on sabbatical leave in 1960 and had written to Monsignor Escrivá requesting that Opus Dei come to Australia. But it was not until an official invitation was issued by the then

Archbishop of Sydney, Cardinal Sir Norman Gilroy, that members finally arrived.

The new arrivals rented a house in Silver St, Randwick, and began to provide spiritual activities including retreats, mainly for university staff and students. Soon after Cardinal Gilroy gave some land (in High St, near the University) which had previously been used for stables. With the help of their first Australian friends the Opus Dei members were able to raise enough money to finance the building of the Nairana Cultural Centre. Opened in 1965 with the help of a small group of university staff members who provided tuition, its main purpose was to help prepare high school students for university.

In the same year, 1965, some women of Opus Dei arrived from the United States, South America and Spain. Soon after Cardinal Gilroy asked Opus Dei to help found the residential college which was to become Warrane on land provided by the university. The old Nairana building became Creston residence for women and Opus Dei was firmly established in Australia. Apart from Warrane and Creston, members of Opus Dei initiated the Dartbrooke study centre at Chatswood and the Westburne study centre at Strathfield, the Kenvale training centre at Lindfield and the Eremeran Club for girls in Lorne Avenue, Killara.

The Dartbrooke centre at Chatswood in Sydney's north, is a study centre for students. Its main aim is to help them develop character and live a spirit of service, partly by giving time to the sick, the old and the lonely. It also helps those who want to develop their faith on an intellectual level. The centre does not involve any kind of membership and those who use it do not form any kind of association.

Westburne study centre is a similar venture. It offers tuition in subjects, study skills and other academic areas not specifically covered by curriculums. It also organises sport, outings and visits to the old and lonely.

The Eremeran club, in Lorne Avenue, Killara, provides tutorials and study guidance for university students and lessons in arts and crafts, and arranges bush walking and horse riding excursions. The Eremeran band competes every year in the Sydney Eisteddfod.

The Kenvale centre trains girls who have completed Year 10 in high school in catering and hospitality. The course is geared to the City and Guilds Certificate, London. Trainees receive standard wages and graduates qualify for jobs in catering and housekeeping including junior management positions in hospitals and leading hotels. Kenvale also provides short courses for hospitality agencies. One of the main aims of the centre, as with similar projects in other countries, is to underline the need to treat housework, even in the family home, as a professional task.

Father Masso commented: "This work at home should never be seen as second class work. This does not mean a woman should only work at home. But nevertheless it is important for women who get married to recognise the tremendous importance of their home activities and that they should always take a professional attitude to them. Women who work in the home should never have an inferiority complex. They can be well prepared to do a job with dignity at the same time using their initiative, intelligence and creativity. That is why the women of Opus Dei make a special effort to have initiative in this area, because it is an area people tend to forget and women find themselves without the background to do a good job."

The corporate works of Opus Dei in Australia support

themselves in the same way as those in other countries. The founder of Opus Dei once outlined how they were financed for the New York Times: "Each centre is financed in the same way as any other of its type. Student residences, for example, with the room and board of the residents, high schools with the pupils' tuition, agricultural schools with the sale of their products. But these funds are hardly ever sufficient to cover all the expenses of a centre, especially considering that (Opus Dei's) activities are all planned with an apostolic outlook and that the majority of them are designed for people with very limited economic resources, who in many cases pay only a nominal fee for the training they receive.

"Another important source of funds is the members of Opus Dei who donate part of the money they earn through their professional work. But most important of all is the generous support of many who do not belong to Opus Dei but want to contribute to these social and educational undertakings. The personnel in charge make an effort to arouse an apostolic zeal and a social concern which will move many people to collaborate actively. Since the centres are run with a high degree of professional competence and are planned to meet real needs of the community, in most cases the response has been very generous. You probably know, for example, that the Association of Friends of the University of Navarre has some 12,000 members. The finances of each centre are autonomous. They are run on an independent basis and look for ways to find the necessary funds among people interested in their activities."

Today the members of Opus Dei in Australia number about 300. They include nine priests—Father Masso, Father Frank Garcia, Father Rom Josko, Fr Victor Martinez, Fr Jerry Gehringer, Fr John Flader, Fr Max Polak, Fr Paul Grant and

Fr Tony Khoudair. Most members do not work in corporate works of Opus Dei. They include representatives of most professions from scientists and academics to carpenters and hairdressers. Some members have helped develop schools. Two of these are the Tangara school for girls in Sydney's north-western suburb of Cherrybrook and the Redfield boys' school at Wahroonga. Both schools are based on the Church's teaching that parents are the primary educators of their children and encourage close links between home and school. The chaplains at both schools are priests of Opus Dei, although it is clear that those who run the schools are responsible for them, not Opus Dei.

Many of the attacks on Opus Dei launched overseas, including the claims that it is a secret society and has worldly ambitions have filtered through to Australia. This publicity has to date occupied an inordinate proportion of the "testimony of others" in Australia. The claims of secrecy and worldliness have already been treated at length. However there is a further allegation levelled at Opus Dei that its members use extreme penance.

The truth of the matter is Opus Dei has no teachings of its own in this area. Its members simply follow the teachings of the Church. As ordinary Catholics they are free to decide matters like this for themselves.

No-one has ever suggested members of Opus Dei have used any penance to excess or that anyone has done themselves harm in any way. Most importantly, in Opus Dei the emphasis is on moderation; not on big things but small things. The preferred mortifications are those which involve putting up with the discomforts caused by other people in every day life. Self-imposed penances might include restricting yourself to two beers instead of three, missing the football in order to take the family on an outing, and so on—all small things which help a person to live a more Christian life.

To my own knowledge there is a reluctance in Opus Dei to approve demanding penances. It is very difficult, for instance, to get permission to fast for any length of time. The emphasis is on a change of heart, not on enduring great discomforts. The general spirit in Opus Dei is reflected in point 173 of The Way which says: "The appropriate word you left unsaid; the joke you didn't tell; the cheerful smile for those who bother you; that silence when you're unjustly accused; your kind conversation with people you find boring and tactless; the daily effort to overlook one irritating detail or another in those who live with you . . . this, with perseverence, is indeed solid interior mortification."

Another claim highlighted in Australia is the one that Opus Dei has been responsible for creating divisions in some families. One of the things which stood out during my travels was the great emphasis Opus Dei places on strengthening the family. A good deal has already been covered which reflects Opus Dei's concern for the family and the rights of parents. To complete the picture I spoke to several Australians about the effect of Opus Dei on their families.

Mr John Faehrmann is the principal of a Sydney public school. One of his three sons, Chris, who came into contact with Opus Dei through Warrane College, has been a numerary member for more than 10 years. "When Chris started getting involved he told me straight away," Mr Faehrmann said. "Later when he decided to become a member he came along once again and told me face to face and explained Opus Dei as well as he could. There was no attempt at concealment. In fact he gave me a copy of The Way which I read from cover to cover.''

Mr Faehrmann said he and his wife had been happy with the effect Chris's membership had had on him. "Before he seemed to be all over the place," he said. "But after he was more settled. When Opus Dei has been criticised my wife, Morna, has commented: 'Well it never led my boys astray.' "

"Chris comes home to family occasions whenever he can. I think sometimes Morna has been a bit disappointed because Chris has not come home as often as she would have liked but when he does he quite charms her. She appreciates the complete attention she gets.''

Perhaps the best endorsement of the effect of Opus Dei on his son is the fact that Mr Faehrmann himself has become a member, as has another of his sons, Peter. There are many people like John Faehrmann who not only approve of their children's involvement in Opus Dei, but are enthusiastic about it (from my experience it would be surprising if they accounted for less than 99 per cent of parents). Some have spoken publicly when Opus Dei has been under attack in the media.

One of these is Mrs Rosheen Limbers, who came into contact with Opus Dei soon after it came to Australia. Though not a member herself, several of her eight children are members and her 17 year-old son, John, is a regular at the Dartbrooke study centre. The study centre organises hikes, camps and study weekends, teaches mechanics, aero modelling, carpentry, and how to develop good study habits and offers members a chance to mix with boys from different backgrounds and schools. It also encourages a spirit of service: in early 1987 the boys spent their school holidays in Papua New Guinea helping to renovate and paint homes of disabled men and their families. Above all, say those who run the club, it is a service to parents who are encouraged to call regularly and to take part in decisions involving their children.

Mrs Limbers said she had come to view the Study Centre like a "friend of the family": "Teenagers get a lot of buffeting from their environment these days, and to have a place like the club where they get clear ideas and where they are motivated is a big help," she said. "They hear these higher ideals, things like service and industriousness and all the rest of it. And they see it being lived by others of their age and it has a great effect. John, for instance, has changed in the last 12 months. He is more outgoing and takes more of an interest in others. The encouragement he has received in the club is something that can't be given in the family; children tend to get so bogged down with their relationship to all the others in the family. Having a person outside with their interests at heart is absolutely invaluable.

"My husband, Paul, who is not a Catholic, feels the same way. We have always felt we could trust the children going to centers of Opus Dei one hundred percent. The fruits of them going there have been unmistakable. They have been happier and much better in both the practice of their faith and in the ordinary things of life, like getting themselves organised, and many of the little things which make life much more pleasant in the family."

Mrs Limbers said members of Opus Dei had provided most of her children's religious instruction over the years. She said she valued most the help she was given to respect her children's freedom, especially when some of them stopped practising their faith. "If I hadn't had the support of people in Opus Dei I don't think I could have done it," she said.

"I would have felt too threatened. I needed someone to tell me it was very wrong to try to take away a person's freedom, that it was not my business even though as a mother I was obviously interested and concerned. I wouldn't have known that that was right somehow. I wouldn't have known there was something of higher importance and that it was their freedom. I think that was the most sterling contribution I have had from Opus Dei. And as it turned out almost all the children have come back to their faith."

Mrs Limbers spoke of past criticism of Opus Dei in the media. "It upset me that people could misunderstand because for me the spirit of Opus Dei is beautifully human. When it has been criticised I have been at pains to put things right. I have never heard a coherent argument against Opus Dei. They are usually very emotional. The most frequent one is this thing of secrecy. Interestingly enough, the people pressing this have not wanted to know the truth. They really don't want to know what Opus Dei is. But many people see the good in it, and that more than balances out the misunderstanding."

Paul and Angela Quinn, originally from Sydney, had been living in Hobart for three years. Paul is a musician and Angela, now a full-time housewife, is a trained speech therapist. Angela joined Opus Dei when she was 19. Paul is not a member. I asked him what it was like being married to a member?

"In the first three years I suppose I was critical of Angela's tremendous devotion to spiritual things," he said. "Maybe it was like a father getting jealous about the first child: I was jealous about the time Angela had for Opus Dei. It annoyed me that she prayed every day, went to mass and the rest. But over the years I have learned to cope with all that.

"In fact I have helped to organise several retreats and recollections given by priests of Opus Dei in Hobart. Going to their (Opus Dei's) recollections I have been left with the impression that if a man was to listen to all the practical advice and put it into practice you would certainly have a good marriage.

"I think as I have grown up with my family I can look and see more of the quality within Opus Dei because of what it stands for in society. On one hand Opus Dei is so family conscious. And on the other hand society is less and less so. The family is becoming a nonentity. That Opus Dei is not conforming to this trend I would say is one of the reasons why it would not be as popular today as it would have been 30 years ago.

"I suppose one other thing I have found attractive is that all the members I have met have a quality of sincerity and that is something which is very rare these days. I mean you meet these young people with families and they are so happy. They have their feet solidly on the ground and they never complain. When you meet someone 60 or 70 times and they are always happy and friendly you realise it is not something put on, that it is natural. It was the sincerity which impressed me.

Paul said he would like to be a member of Opus Dei himself. "But I know how demanding it is," he said and I could only do it if I felt I could do it justice."

Finally Noel Ling, the former bursar of Warrane College, had some comments to make on the claim that Opus Dei takes "children" away from their parents (children here meaning people 18 years and over). "Friends have asked me about these claims," he said. "Obviously no parent wants their child to be taken away from them but it is a fact of life. You only have a loan of your children for a short time. When they grow up they are taken away from you in one way or another. If a person decided to become a priest or a nun and their parents were not Christians and did not have an understanding of Catholic Church they would be very mad about the whole thing. They would see it as having their children taken away from them.

"In the Protestant Church in Asia we have a tremendous amount of this sort of complaint because Buddhist parents complain the Christian Church has taken their children away. In Singapore, Hong Kong and Indonesia it happens all the time. It is not that children get taken away it is that children want to leave and have decided that for themselves. So far as Opus Dei is concerned they cannot be accused of doing anything. It is the children themselves who make their own decisions. I can understand Opus Dei's point of view. And I can understand that this is not possible to explain to a television interviewer who does not want to listen.

"This is one of the things I point out to my Protestant friends when they ask me why I am involved in Opus Dei. I simply tell them it is because I want to do God's work. Opus Dei means 'work of God' and the members I know are very sincere and I find they do want to do God's work, passionately."

11

CONCLUSION

I T had been a long journey, taking in 10 countries and dozens of projects and touching on the lives of thousands of people. But given the size and scope of Opus Dei it was barely a beginning. At the outset I had planned to go to France, Germany and Peru, but it was not possible. In Peru I had hoped to see Piura University where wealthier students are subsidising the education of the poor. There was also the direct work with Peru's poor, helping them to improve their general education and to learn modern agricultural methods.

Even though there were many more places to visit, I believe I have nevertheless succeeded in what I set out to do, to convey something of the spirit of Opus Dei. Reflecting on the journey now that it was over I realised how well Opus

Dei fitted both into the ordinary life of men and women
living in the world and into the life of the Church. I could
appreciate better Monsignor Escrivá's belief that it could be
said "without any kind of arrogance, but with gratitude to
the goodness of God", that Opus Dei would never have any
problems adapting to the world, that it would never find
itself in need of being brought up to date. God, he argued,
had put Opus Dei up to date once and for all when he gave
it its lay characteristics. "It will never need to adapt itself
to the world," he said, "because all its members are of the
world."

To see how well the Prelature of Opus Dei fits into the
Catholic Church, one needs to go no further than the
documents of the Second Vatican Council. The same spirit
that animates Opus Dei can be seen throughout these
documents. The following are just a few passages which
could be quoted:

On work the council says: "Those who engage in human
work, often of a heavy kind, should perfect themselves
through it, help their fellow-citizens, and promote the
betterment of the whole of human society and the whole
of creation; indeed, with their active charity, rejoicing in
hope and bearing one another's burdens, they should imitate
Christ who plied his hands with carpenter's tools and is
always working with the Father for the salvation of all; and
they should rise to a higher sanctity, truly apostolic, by their
everyday work itself . . . Therefore all the faithful are invited
and obliged to holiness and the perfection of their own state
of life."

On the apostolate of lay people the council says: "The
Church was founded to spread the kingdom of Christ over
all the earth for the glory of God the Father to make all men

partakers in redemption and salvation, and through them to establish the right relationship of the entire world to Christ. Every activity of the Mystical Body with this in view goes by the name of "apostolate'; the Church exercised it through all its members, though in various ways. In fact, the Christian vocation is, of its nature, a vocation to the apostolate as well.''

It is clear that Opus Dei is not, as some people have tried to argue, a "sect" or a "trend" or a movement of conservatives, but a part of the constitutional structure of the Catholic Church. It has an official standing equal, though different to, that of the territorial diocese. Certainly Opus Dei has been criticised. But in a sense even that can be considered in its favor, for Christ taught that the servant would be treated no better than the master. While being criticised is not in itself a proof that Opus Dei is divinely inspired, it is nevertheless what you would expect of something loyal to the teachings of Christ.

Perhaps the strongest impression I gained during the journey was that the "spirit" of Opus Dei was not a vague generalisation, but a real and palpable thing. Everywhere I went people lived much the same spiritual regimen. They prayed, received the sacraments, tried to sanctify their work and so on. But this spirit which united them expressed itself in many different ways. It was not just that people engaged in different professions felt they were able to use those different professions to go to God, that a professor could use his work to be a contemplative, just as a gardener or a taxi driver could. This in itself was interesting, but what caught my imagination was the different projects members of Opus Dei were involved in from country to country and even within the same country.

While in one place the spirit of Opus Dei expressed itself in a language school, in another it inspired an agricultural school and in a third schools which fought racial discrimination. In one country members of Opus Dei taught people to raise chickens, in another they taught businessmen to be good economists. In Japan Opus Dei tried to get people not to work so much; in Mexico it encouraged them to work harder. In one country, Spain, you could see members operating on so many different levels—training both farmers and academics, establishing a university, schools and youth clubs, building a hospital in one place, a magnificent shrine in another, helping the disabled to live with dignity and so on. In one city, Rome, you could see the diversity in an even smaller setting with Centro ELIS carrying out so many necessary functions in a community which formerly lacked the most basic social institutions.

All of this argues against the view that Opus Dei is something rigid and authoritarian. On the contrary, its dynamism and ability to respond to so many different needs in so many different situations is the fruit of freedom. No strictly controlled organisation could ever have such results, only one firmly grounded in encouraging the freedom of the individual.

Finally, although the journey had offered many insights into its nature, I believe any attempt to capture the spirit of Opus Dei in words must necessarily be inadequate. I can sympathise with those who sincerely believe it is a secret society, not because Opus Dei is secret, but because I believe in the final analysis it is a mystery. Its appearance, growth and success are all mysterious. It can be argued they are so because they are part of the mystery that is the Church, a mystery which has survived now for almost 2000 years.

CONCLUSION

At the heart of this mystery is something very simple, something so simple that the sophisticated 20th Century often finds it difficult to grasp. It is not something new so much as something which sheds new light on things that have always been there—on ordinary life, the family, work, friendship and the service of God. The following quote from the founder of Opus Dei encapsulates this thing he spoke of repeatedly throughout his life, a life dedicated to spreading Opus Dei, the work of God

"I dream—and the dream has come true—of multitudes of God's children, sanctifying themselves as ordinary citizens, sharing the ambitions and endeavours of their colleagues and friends. I want to shout to them about this divine truth: if you are there in the middle of ordinary life, it doesn't mean Christ has forgotten about you or hasn't called you. He has invited you to stay among the activities and concerns of the world. He wants you to know that your human vocation, your profession, your talents, are not omitted from his divine plans. He has sanctified them and made them a most acceptable offering to His Father."

APPENDIX

FOLLOWING are some basic details about Opus Dei, its founder and its history.

First Personal Prelature

Opus Dei is the Catholic Church's first personal prelature, a body which is not (like a parish) limited to a particular territory. Initiated by the Second Vatican Council, personal prelatures are designed to allow priests and lay people to carry out particular pastoral tasks without being restricted to a particular district or area.

Opus Dei became a personal prelature in 1982 following an extensive three and a half year, world wide study of all aspects of its operations by the Sacred Congregation of

Bishops. (At this inquiry bishops in all countries where Opus Dei had operated were invited to make submissions about its activities.) Established in 1928, Opus Dei had already received juridical approval from the Church on several occasions. It was made a secular institute in 1947 and its statutes were approved by the Church in 1950. But before 1982 its legal status, that of a "secular institute", was considered to be like a badly fitting suit of clothes. Among other things the status of Personal Prelature made it more clear that Opus Dei's faithful are ordinary Christian lay people and secular priests.

Spirituality

When Monsignor Escrivá began to preach the spirituality of Opus Dei it fitted in well with the direction of the Church of the time. In the late 1920s the Church had been moved for some time to turn its attention to the role of lay people. The Popes had been writing about social questions, highlighting basic Christian principles to guide those active in political, economic and social life. In some countries, notably France and Italy, co-operatives, banks and even political parties had been founded on these principles. At the same time prominent Catholic thinkers, such as the French philosopher, Jacques Maritain, had been devoting their energies to the subject of religion and social questions. Don Josemaría was obviously aware of these developments. But, as he said, his action in founding Opus Dei had its inspiration elsewhere. It was not the result of an ongoing debate or an intellectual movement. It was based on what he believed was a direct call from God.

APPENDIX

There had been other attempts to develop spiritualities for lay people, as distinct from those for religious who live apart from "the world". And the key that Monsignor Escriva proposed for lay people to seek sanctity—everyday work—had always had a place in the church's teaching. There are many texts from scripture which point to the importance of work. For instance Genesis says God made man "ut operaretur", "in order to work". And spiritual writers like St Augustine mentioned the value of work. "I will teach you a way to praise God all day long," Augustine wrote. "Whenever you do something, do it well and you will have praised God."

But even though there were many isolated references to the Christian meaning of work, a spirituality had not yet been built around it. The monks had always placed a great value on work, but they saw it from the viewpoint of religious, not that of ordinary people living in secular society. One of the Church's great spiritual writers, Saint Francis de Sales, had devoted much attention to the lay person, but he spoke little of ordinary work. As Cardinal Albino Luciani pointed out in an article one month before he became Pope John Paul I: "Monsignor Escriva went further than Francis de Sales in many respects. Saint Francis proclaimed sanctity for everyone but seems to have taught only a 'spirituality for lay people' whereas Monsignor Escrivá wants a 'lay spirituality'." "Saint Francis," added Cardinal Luciani, "suggests the same practical means as used by religious, but with suitable modifications."

The spirituality of Opus Dei is based on the concept of ordinary people trying to imitate the life of Christ as a worker. Simply put, its mission amounts to two words: "Be

Yourself''. Its teaching is that, if you are a baker, then you should make being a baker a central part of your search for spiritual growth. If you are a Prime Minister, then you should make being a Prime Minister a central part of your spiritual life. Members are urged to carry out apostolate—a term which simply means spreading the Gospel—as a central part of their vocation. They try to communicate to their friends, relatives and acquaintances the Church's universal call for every human being to strive for sanctity, particularly by offering their daily work to God.

This spirit, which is firmly rooted in the Gospel, explains Opus Dei's quick growth in so many countries. It has already left a strong mark in the Church. The importance of the universal call to holiness and sanctification through ordinary work is heavily emphasised in the solemn documents of the Second Vatican Council. The central feature of this spirit is to transform ordinary work into a means for seeking sanctity and doing apostolate. This is achieved through doing work as well as possible in order to offer it to God and for the good of society and the service of others. It involves exercising virtues like charity, justice, diligence, cheerfulness, order and loyalty. The faithful of the prelature practice daily prayer, daily mass and holy communion, reading the Gospel and spiritual books, mostly small penances (such as forgoing some small amount of food), weekly confession, a yearly spiritual retreat, regular courses in theology and so on.

Each member (there are about 80,000) receives regular spiritual direction. This involves an informal discussion of how their spiritual life is developing. Each one can take up any matter affecting their spiritual life. However any advice given in regard to family or professional life relates exclusively to Christian morals. No member is ever given advice on how to solve specific problems. Members receive regular instruction in Catholic doctrine (Opus Dei has no doctrine or school of thought of its own) and each one contributes whatever they can afford to help support corporate apostolates.

Monsignor Escrivá once explained the spirituality of Opus Dei in the following way: "We have reminded Christians of the wonderful words of Genesis which tell us that God created man so that he might work, and have concentrated on the example of Christ, who spent most of his life on earth working as a craftsman in a village. We love human work which he chose as his state in life, and which he cultivated and sanctified. We see in work, in men's noble creative toil, not only one of the highest human values, an indispensable means to social progress and to greater justice in the relations between men, but also a sign of God's love for his creatures, and of men's love for each other and for God: we see in work a means of perfection, a way to sanctity. Hence the sole objective of Opus Dei has always been to see that there be men and women of all races and social conditions who endeavour to love and to serve God and the rest of mankind in and through their ordinary work, in the midst of the realities and interests of the world."

Corporate Works

Corporate works include schools, universities, study centres, youth clubs, medical dispensaries, student residences and training centres for workers, all of which aim to satisfy some social need, to promote justice in society. These involve relatively few members. Opus Dei does not own these works, it merely provides the spiritual care, guaranteeing at the same time that all the instruction given there is in line with the teachings of the Catholic Church. Corporate works are not "ecclesiastical activities" representing the hierarchy of the Church. Ordinary people, including non-Catholics, take care of planning, development, day-to-day running, finance, hiring and firing and relations with civil and ecclesiastical authorities.

The founder of Opus Dei explained corporate works this way: "These centres are undoubtedly sources which project the Christian view of life. Run by laypeople, directed as professional activities by lay citizens who are the same as their colleagues at work, and open to people of all classes and conditions, these centres have made many sectors of society appreciate the need of offering a Christian solution to the problems which arise in the exercise of their profession or job."

The founder added: "Opus Dei, whose aims are exlusively spiritual, can only carry out corporatively activities which clearly constitute an immediate Christian service, as an apostolate. It would be ridiculous to think that Opus Dei as such could mine coal or run any type of commercial venture. Its corporate works are all directly apostolic activities . . . in other words, educational or welfare activities like those carried on throughout the world by organisations of every religious creed."

In addition to the corporate works, individual members are encouraged to start up their own social projects they consider to be useful to society as a whole. Again they include medical dispensaries, schools and institutions to help the poor. The fact that one or more members of Opus Dei are involved does not mean Opus Dei is responsible for these projects. If a request is made a priest of Opus Dei may be appointed as chaplain, but Opus Dei takes responsibility only for the priest's activity, not for any other aspect of the project. The founder of Opus Dei believed that lay people should never present themselves as representing the Church. He believed lay people, after familiarising themselves with the teachings of the Church, should act with personal freedom and responsibility, without pretending that their's was the "Catholic solution" to a problem or the "Catholic way" of acting. Over the years some people who have misunderstood Opus Dei have interpreted this approach as a way of disguising Opus Dei's involvement in different projects. These people overlook the fundamental importance the founder placed on freedom and responsibility. For Monsignor Escrivá this emphasis on freedom and responsibility was crucial.

Membership

Opus Dei's central offices are at 75 Viale Bruno Buozzi in Rome. The prelature is headed by an elected Prelate, Monsignor Alvaro del Portillo, and divided into regions governed by regional vicars, appointed by the Prelate and assisted by their councils. Regions may be subdivided into delegations governed by a vicar delegate (a priest), also assisted by councils. Opus Dei members are either priests or lay people, the priests being drawn exclusively from among lay members. Most members are married and are from all social groups and occupations. They remain ordinary lay Catholics under the jurisdiction of their local bishop. They enter into a simple contract, committing themselves to strive for sanctity in their work, to help spread this ideal and to assist with the apostolic tasks of the prelature, while the prelature commits itself to provide the assistance necessary to pursue these goals.

The minimum age of an Opus Dei member is 18. At that age a person can make a commitment for 12 months. This commitment must be renewed at least five times over a period of five years before any permanent commitment can be made.

Members may be:

Numeraries: priests or lay people with a vocation to live celibacy so that they can concentrate more fully on teaching the faith or to help with special apostolates. They normally live in a centre of Opus Dei so that they can make themselves completely available for activities like teaching doctrine and giving spiritual advice.

Associates: lay people who also live celibacy and carry out similar tasks to numeraries but normally live with their own families due to long-term personal, family or professional needs. (The priests incardinated in Opus Dei are drawn exclusively from the prelature's own numeraries and associates.)

Supernumeraries: lay men and women, either single or married, who take part in the apostolates of Opus Dei in a way which is compatible with their family, professional and social commitments. They also try to live the same spirit of sanctifying work and apostolate as other faithful of the prelature.

(For everyone who belongs to Opus Dei, the vocation is the same. Each member takes up the same ascetical and educational commitments in a way that fits their family circumstances. There are no different classes among the members; the different names—numeraries, associates, and

APPENDIX

supernumeraries—refer only to different personal situations and to the different availability of those who join the prelature.)

Cooperators: not members of Opus Dei, but people who help its apostolic activities with prayers, donations, gifts and sometimes with direct assistance.

Associates Priest: priests who are already ordained, but join Opus Dei as members of what is known as the Priestly Society of the Holy Cross. This is an association of priests united to the prelature. Its aim is to spread the spirit of Opus Dei among the secular clergy. The prelate of Opus Dei is the president of the society which includes both priests incaradinated in Opus Dei and other secular priests who continue being incardinated in their own dioceses and under the exclusive jurisdiction of their own bishop. The society is therefore an association which promotes the sanctity of priests. These associations were praised by the Second Vatican Council in the Decree on the Ministry and Life of Priests. Priests of the society pursue sanctity, through their ordinary work—that is their priestly ministry while the society provides spiritual and ascetical care which encourages them, among other things, to be completely available to their Bishop and diocese.

Publications

Among the best known writings of the founder of Opus Dei is a book of personal spiritual reflections based on the Gospel, The Way. It has been published in 192 editions in 36 languages with a total print run of more than 3 million copies. Other publications include: Furrow and The Forge (further spiritual reflections), Holy Rosary (short meditations),

OPUS DEI

Conversations with Monsignor Escriva (a collection of interviews with newspapers and magazines including Time, Le Figaro and the New York Times), Christ is Passing By and Friends of God (both books of homilies), and The Way of the Cross (meditations). Many films were made of public meetings at which Monsignor Escriva answered the questions of hundreds of thousands of people around the world. The prelature publishes Romana, a bulletin with news on the church and Opus Dei, twice a year.

INDEX

INDEX

INDEX

INDEX